Dedication

To a supportive editorial team that worked with me to make this book possible: Specifically, publisher Dorothy Harris, who spontaneously believed in the power of music and became my sounding board to make sure the complexities of music therapy were translated into "user-friendly" formats; and editor/co-writer Kate McLoughlin, whose voracious love for music and journalism transformed my music therapy knowledge into practical information that is (hopefully!) easily understood.

To the loving arms and understanding nature of my husband, Dr. Dennis Burkhardt, for my endless nights at the computer/fax and time spent away from home; and to our four wonderful, supportive children in our blended family—Tom, Meghan, Tim, and Michael.

To my finest friends, especially in St. George, Las Vegas, and Anchorage, who provided my support network and spiritual food over the decades. Recently, Connie and John, Bob and Betty, Karen and Richard, Gary and Patricia, Donna, Alan, and Joe.

To my roots—Frank and Carol Pinkerton, who agreed to bring me into this world to experience music at its finest with my four siblings, Gary, Nancy, Jim, and Dan, and to our extended family in Colorado and beyond.

I gratefully acknowledge the many people who have shared their observations with me, facilitated through music therapy workshops, counseling sessions, research, and interviews. Finally, over all, thanksgiving to God for all experiences that have made this healing opportunity possible!

The Sound of Healing

CREATE YOUR OWN MUSIC PROGRAM FOR BETTER HEALTH

Judith Pinkerton

Alliance Publishing, Inc.

ISBN 1-887110-00-3

Cover and Interior Design by Cynthia Dunne
Produced by Publisher's Studio, Albany, New York
Alliance Books are available at
special discounts for bulk purchase for sales promotions,
premiums, fund raising, or educational use.
For details, contact:
Alliance Publishing, Inc.
P.O. Box 080377
Brooklyn, New York 11208-0002

Distributed to the trade by National Book Network, Inc.
10 8 6 4 2 1 3 5 6 7 9

Grateful acknowledgment is made for permission to reprint the following:

"Finder of Lost Loves," by Burt Bacharach and Carol Bayer Sager. © Copyright
1985, New Hidden Valley Music, Carol Bayer Sager Music, Spelling Ventures
Music, SVO Music. International copyright secured. All rights reserved. Reprinted
with permission.

"The Thunder Rolls," by Garth Brooks and Pat Alger. Reprint permission by
Major Bob Music Co., Inc. (ASCAP)/Bait & Beer Music/Forerunner Music, Inc.
(ASCAP). © Copyright 1988. All rights reserved. Reprinted with permission.

"The Music of The Night," from THE PHANTOM OF THE OPERA. Music by
Andrew Lloyd Webber. Lyrics by Charles Hart. Additional lyrics by Richard Stil-
goe. © Copyright 1986, The Really Useful Group Ltd. All rights for the United
States and Canada administered by Polygram International Publishing, Inc. International copyright secured. All rights reserved. Reprinted with permission.

"Let the Beat Control Your Body," by 2 Unlimited and writers P. Wilde, F.
Martens, R. L. Slijngaard, A. D. Dels. Any Kind of Music, Inc./Decos Music.©
Copyright 1993. All rights reserved. Reprinted with permission.

"Practice Makes Perfect," by Michael Franks. Mississippi Mud Music (BMI).©
Copyright 1993. All rights reserved. Reprinted with permission.

Every effort has been made to locate and credit the copyright holders of material
quoted in this book.

Table of Contents

Prelude

Music is the shorthand of emotion. Emotions which let themselves be described in words with such difficulty are directly conveyed to man in music, and in that is its power and significance.

—LEO TOLSTOY (1828–1910)

How could music possibly relieve my anxiety when I was looking at an airplane propeller that had stopped rotating and I was 900 feet above the ground?

Time passed in a matter of seconds as the airplane dove for the ground. There was no time to use music. In the aftermath, however, music could have reduced my high anxiety, which exploded into anger. Music that followed a special sequence, initially matching my anxiety and anger, followed by more peaceful, then happier, music. I now believe that this kind of music sequencing could have brought my anxiety and anger under control within fifteen minutes.

What music would make me feel better about my boyfriend, who left me for another woman?

I was frantic to salvage our love, not willing to let him go. If I had listened to a music tape similarly sequenced as the one above whenever I felt frantic, I could have released that relationship in a matter of days instead of weeks.

Why don't more people like classical music? I was frustrated by this when the growth of the talent agency I had created, which represented only classical ensembles, plateaued, stopped growing. Thus, I started promoting other styles of music—country, bluegrass, and jazz, as well as rock 'n' roll. The musicians I dealt with were fascinating, talented people. Looking back, I now think that because I loosened up my attitudes, business for my classical musicians improved as well. It didn't occur to me at the time that I had been limiting my own musical world, that my beliefs had begun to subtly change. It seemed to be just a business decision.

I've listened to and booked all styles of music. I'm also a professional musician. I was familiar with a wide range of music at an intellectual, professional level, but I wasn't a therapist at that time. It had not occurred to me that I could use music effectively to better my health. Eventually, I intuitively used music to help someone else and that experience began the learning process that has changed my life. It taught me what, where, when, and how to use music for better health. It taught me what I am now sharing with you—that the world of music we take for granted can become *The Sound of Healing*.

That initial incident took place nine years ago, during a previous marriage. My husband had required emergency back surgery. We had discovered in the months prior to his surgery that when I played my violin for him at night, he would sleep soundly and wake up without the usual back pain, and would have no need for medication. I played the music he loved to hear—Irish medleys and easy listening, as well as the more challenging classical pieces I liked to play, however, I kept those mellow.

The night before his surgery, I recorded a one-hour tape of my husband's favorites, something he would enjoy listening to after surgery. When he returned to his hospital room, groggy but awake, I immediately put the headphones on his ears and turned on the portable cassette player. The nurse came by every fifteen minutes thereafter to monitor his vital signs. Thirty minutes had passed when she returned with her hypodermic needle to administer the postsurgical high blood pressure medication. As she checked his vital signs she looked at the headphones, frowned, and whipped around. "What is he listening to?" she demanded. "Me," I replied timidly. "What do you mean 'me'?" she queried, somewhat upset. "I play the violin. That's me on the tape," I answered. I was embarrassed because the tape wasn't a professional recording.

She responded, "This is impossible. I'm supposed to be giving him medication right now and he doesn't need it!" So I asked, "Isn't that good?" The nurse thought about it and said, "Yes . . . can I have a copy of that tape?" Then she noted in his medical records that music instead of medication had been used. It didn't occur to me to ask about his pain level because I was not involved in music therapy at the time, and I had no idea that music could have an effect on pain. All I remember is what my husband told me—that an overwhelming sense of peace and well-being came over him while listening to the music.

It is my hope that the information in this book and the techniques for creating your own health-based music program may help deepen your sense of peace and well-being, expand your capacity to experience love, joy, enthusiasm, and happiness, and control or diminish your anxiety, anger, depression, or grief. The stories herein come from people across the country who have been experiencing such renewal.

The potential combinations of music that can be used to better your physical and psychological health are limitless. New recordings are released daily. This also breeds confusion, as there is so much from which to choose. Also, what worked for your friend won't necessarily work for you. The solution lies in discovering what to look for and when to listen to it. *The Sound of Healing* focuses on health-effective music listening, and explains what to buy and why, and what to do and when. You will learn, simply and effectively, how to build a music collection for therapeutic benefit.

Annotating and broadening your music library will help you find selections that connect to anxiety, love, or energy and meet the changing demands you face in emotional and physical health. My desire is that you USE™ this book—USE being the acronym for the method that will help you develop the program that is right for you. The knowledge gained from the book will reinforce your own intuitive knowledge and personal music preferences. I came to learn the same truth myself: Music is a health resource we often don't appreciate, one which can surely help us find new ways to help ourselves and others.

— Judith Pinkerton

Music's

Power

to Heal:

MYSTERY AND COMMON SENSE

1

One New Way to Listen,

Many
Ways to
Heal

THE WAY MUSIC works on the human mind for emotional and physiological healing remains part mystery, part scientific knowledge,
and part common sense. Solving the mystery is the realm of psychological and medical research. The common sense part is what
we may understand on an intuitive level, since turning to music is
often what people do first, before considering counseling, meditation, or even talking to friends. Whether we are agitated, angry,
miserable, or bored, music follows close to prayer in terms of what
we turn to intuitively, hoping it can help or at least provide a distraction. What is seldom dealt with is how powerful the effect of
music actually is, and whether you might be able to engage that
power for healing.

"Maybe music can keep your mind off things for awhile, but it
can't make any real difference." "I never notice what music is playing anyway." These are two opinions I've heard a lot; they are as
common as they are wrong. If music is playing somewhere within
your ears' range, whether you've chosen it or not, whether you are
consciously aware of the sound or not, you *are* being affected.

More than just a distraction, music can be a gently powerful agent of relief in dealing with an emotional problem. The sound of healing is a very real concept. My work as a music therapist has convinced me that music helps people in physical pain, not just by taking their minds off the pain, but by actively affecting the condition of pain.

A music therapist can design a therapeutic music program which adapts music therapy techniques to individual needs, dealing with the type of pain and the individual's history. Pain relief, aided by an expert or self-generated, becomes possible when you evoke emotions that oppose the emotions that go along with pain, since one cannot experience two emotional states at the same time.[1] There is also evidence that music directly stimulates the body's own internal chemical pain relievers. This idea will be developed on a personal healing level throughout the book, through individual stories which may have meaning in your own life.

To the extent you've collected any music at all, or you listen to music regularly, something has already been going on between your music, your body, and your mind. You probably already have the material to accomplish good results; now, how do you use it to maximum effect as a health resource? By understanding what in your favorite music makes it your favorite, you will discover new music to give you increased benefits and how to choose the exact music to deal with your specific problem.

It's likely that your music library consists of some works that are genuinely valuable to you, albums that you used to like, "important" pieces you feel you ought to own or like, the too-expensive-to-throw-away results of other peoples' recommendations, and gifts from friends and lovers. Can you find in this assortment certain works and then certain segments of those works that legitimately improve the way you feel? Yes, and you can build your collection more effectively.

In any given situation, you may get lucky. Six times out of ten you may find just the music that works for you at the moment, suiting the mood and situation. But the other four times your intuition may need some help. Achieving that comes through understanding what in music opens the avenue to healing and what in you responds. Certain music, and single elements within many kinds of music, trigger responses, responses below the conscious level. *Rhythm* and *melody* may be the first things you notice about music, but there are eight more elements in the ten building blocks of any piece of music, from rock to Rachmaninoff; these elements cue psychological and physiological responses.

For instance, *pitch* (the frequency of a sound wave) stimulates cellular circuits within the brain. Those circuits "recognize" high and low frequencies and patterns of pitches, and it is that cellular recognition level that makes songs and melodies "familiar" or "easy to remember."[2] Added to this are the myriad emotional connections, positive and negative, which you, as an individual with your own life history, bring to music. Which of these factors, together or separately, consciously or not, you react to will be explained, along with the fundamentals of a system for accurately matching music to your moods. You can then "tune your body" to produce tranquil meditation, to increase energy, and to decrease stress, pain, anger, grief, depression, or anxiety.

Music at Work

Three elements change when you listen to music: your body, your behavior, and your emotions. All three are interrelated. By "body," I don't mean simply the vibration of sound waves in your ears, but the whole spectrum of what is involved physiologically—hormones, neurotransmitters, heart rate, respiratory rate, and brain wave patterns. The effects of the physical changes are easiest to identify—emotions, pain indicators, and behavior—since they are rooted in your internal architecture, but are visible on the outside. For example:

- You're pushing yourself to increase your athletic endurance—say, in running—but you can't get past that plateau of exhaustion or muscle soreness that keeps you from going any further, any longer. The right music will reach past the weariness, counteract the frustration, encourage your body to move more efficiently, and help you more closely reach your personal best. Muscle movement and respiration seek to match music's tempo and rhythm, to keep pace with the music. Concurrently, the music increases the body's electrochemical activity, which keeps your momentum going.
- You're at home and faced with a cleaning chore you've been putting off forever. If you don't clean, no one will come to visit you. You won't even want to be there yourself. You can

transform this dreaded chore into a challenge, or at least a tolerable experience, with a positive attitude. That positive attitude can come from an internal surge of adrenaline, a revved-up heart rate, and a faster, zap-that-dust technique.

You can reach that high point with music. The same music elements applicable to exercise—tempo and rhythm—may energize your body to keep the cleaning activity going, while the addition of melody and lyrics motivates and gives you positive reinforcement.

- You're working on a business project with a deadline, and no ideas are coming. You not only cannot solve any problems, your brain is fogged over. Tense, tight, teeth gritted, and out of ideas, what do you do? You find a way to focus your concentration, relax your physical tension, and access some of the creative thinking you know is buried within. That means changing your brain wave patterns, among other things. Music can make that happen.

Specific combinations of music elements—certain pitches, slower tempos, a regular rhythm or absence of rhythm—effectively alter states of consciousness, from beta, problem solving or activity-oriented thinking, to alpha, where creative thinking flourishes. A variety of music styles, listened to in a specific sequence, may also help.

- You're numbed from a relationship that has gone horribly, unexpectedly wrong. You can't make it better and though it's over, you can't let go. How can you find long-term peace of mind when a single day seems unbearable?

Too many times we want to bury the hurt, hoping it will go away if ignored or repressed. What happens instead is that the repression adversely affects the body physically, with chest aches and headaches or overstimulation of depression-causing chemicals of the brain. Look for the right music to take the chill out of a cold, hard world, and to slowly, gently soothe an aching heart. Surprisingly, when the music you listen to first matches that chilly feeling, and is then followed by music which creates a peaceful center, healing the hurt may come more easily.

- You're in severe physical discomfort that nothing seems to adequately relieve. Medication, even a heavy-duty prescription, isn't doing the job, and increasing the amount you take would cloud your mind. You want to hang on to your mental alertness, but what good is being alert if the main thing you're aware of is how much you hurt? The power of music can both distract you from your suffering and directly impact the internal pain mechanisms. This connects to the patterns of pain that are similar to emotional trauma.

It is impossible to feel two emotions at exactly the same time.[3] Therefore, when music creates an emotion that opposes the emotion accompanying pain, the pain may be reduced or eliminated for a period of time. Accompanying this, the brain's own natural pain-relieving chemicals become involved.[4] Pain is viciously entwined with depression, anxiety, fear, and tension, thus alleviating the emotional factor has physical benefits as well. As with many medical intricacies, *how* it happens is not fully understood, but *that* it happens is clear.

The healing power of music is a belief as old as the Old Testament, and older, if we look to the good books of other cultures. (Apollo, for example, was the god of both medicine and music.) You can use music like a curative laser beam to cut through pain, misery, and emotional smog. Yet most of us listen to music, switching stations, and buying new CDs or tapes, without any clear idea of what we're looking for and the reason behind it.

Your Music to USE

Now you have the opportunity to review a selection of all styles of music, and to expand your collection to meet your needs. It's an easy extension from liking Broadway show melodies to appreciating opera, but if you like rock, you may also like new country. If you like the gritty voice of rock star legend Janis Joplin, you may also like Melissa Etheridge's rough edge, from the progressive folk genre. If you enjoy Handel's "Hallelujah Chorus," you may clap your hands at the Clark Sisters' gospel "Hallelujah!" You will find that every music style is potentially able to function as a source of healing for you. The code to the sound of healing is the matching of emotional states with specific music.

Most of us know fairly well what radio stations we like to hone in on and what music videos we will sit through. We are likely to have already designated certain kinds of music for certain activities—a heavy beat when driving, classical for concentration, fast rock for running, a dash of Whitney Houston when cooking dinner.

Think about the tough times you've gone through and might face again. When a migraine recurs triple-strength, the music of Handel or Bach might help, as it has helped others, time after time, in research studies. If you are hospitalized, hearing some angelic music, by an earthly harp or violin—not a celestial chorus, might ease some of the anxiety. Do sad songs make you feel lonely? Why, sometimes, don't happy songs make you feel better?

This book suggests three categories of music to help all moods. The acronym USE is a handy way to remember not only the categories but what, fundamentally, makes music work, and how the matching of moods to music will affect the healing process. USE translates as Unsettling, Soothing, and Energizing—the range of emotions you may experience daily, matched to music that stimulates that specific emotion.

Unsettling *Music that jangles nerve ends, bestirs the soul, and blackens a mood.*
Soothing *Music that numbs, calms, or deeply relaxes.*
Energizing *Music that puts physiological and psychological "fizz" into your life.*

To build your therapeutic music library, and to structure the way you deliberately plan music throughout your day, or within a particular situation, the later chapters contain a wealth of information about music in these three categories, constructed to match specific emotional states. To help organize your music collection and your thoughts about that collection, however, some basic emotional components are listed for each USE category in chapter 3. You could add more, to personalize the USE listings according to your own emotional range, or according to the predominant emotions of someone you hope to help. The ability to find the correct music has two focal points: first, understanding your own individual needs and desires, and second, having the right music to access for beneficial mood matching. You may have been looking for peace in all the wrong places.

Mood matching

To change emotional states, as you start the process of mood matching, you will need to wrestle with some negative moods. Much of the work you do to rid yourself of anger, depression, fear and anxiety, and to relax muscle tension, will also contribute to pain relief, since these emotional conditions and the experience of pain are so interconnected. When you choose to focus on the actual pain itself, mood matching goes to another level.

Matching physical pain with visual imagery is a delicate, guided process best assisted by qualified music therapists. Psychologist and music therapist Mark Rider recommends "music that initially matches the person's physical or mental state. Then, through a process known as 'entrainment,' the music is changed to help draw the person out of pain."[5]

This music therapy technique for pain management is called GIM (Guided Imagery & Music). It combines visualizations of scenes of physical disturbances, such as angry waves or volcanoes, with the music that matches the pain. Because this technique requires sensitive guided transitions to Soothing and/or Energizing states, I do not recommend that beginners attempt it. As your ability with mood-matching techniques grows stronger, however, working with Unsettling music becomes an option for the management of your own physical pain. (Personal training in Guided Imagery & Music is available through the Bonny Foundation; see Appendix C, p. 189.)

I will add another caution here, as you seek healing. Pain in all its variants, and the intensity with which any one person will feel pain, are highly individualized situations. If you are confronting physical pain, then, in addition to working with music, you should also be working with knowledgeable, caring medical and therapeutic professionals. Similarly, chronic depression should not be self-treated. Consult a music therapist, social worker, psychologist, psychiatrist, or other health care worker for assistance. I advocate self-help, but in certain circumstances, professional advice should be sought.

Your goal, emotionally and physically, is to accomplish the optimum USE of your favorite (old and new) music to achieve your desired state by doing one or all of three things to your current condition: *satiating*, *neutralizing*, or *changing* it.

Your Starting Point

Analyze the mood you are in, and what's going on in your mind and body now. Give some thought to the physiological and emotional clues to your well-being.

SATIATE

Satiating, or completely satisfying, your current mood means selecting the music that will actually match the mood. This is undoubtedly easier—and more comfortable—to do if the mood you are in (and matching) is peaceful or upbeat. But you have to learn to work directly with a downbeat mood as well. You have to enable the music to work with you, with your current emotional state, not against it or in spite of it.

For example, if a black cloud hangs over your day, and you want to go to sleep or just get on with your life, match the appropriate music in the Unsettling category to your mood, usually for the entire length of the piece, with three minutes being the minimum for therapeutic benefit. You have to "work through" the bad stuff, go to the heart of the mood, wallow in the misery, if you like, to be able to get out of it cleanly, without emotional residue. Only then can you effectively go on to the next stage. Minimal benefit results if you pick the Soothing or Energizing music first, while you are still under that black cloud. While the cloud may temporarily fade to gray, the blackness is likely to come back far too soon.

For pain self-management, satiation follows a different path. You need to match and satiate the moods you hope to reach by using familiar music. The familiarity of the music that makes optimum use of conditioned responses, is especially important in pain relief measures.

If your starting point is a positive situation, and you want to satiate the positive, highlight a good time and keep creative juices sparkling, first decide how it's good—mellowness, vitality, excitement, exultation? Then go to the music that matches, or satiates, that emotion, and listen for at least three minutes. Be careful, though. If you are convinced your mood is fine and you use Soothing or Energizing music, but the music seems boring or aggravating, you had better rethink your position. Is it truly positive? Is excitement happiness or is it the high-wiredness of stress? Are you relaxed or are you repressing anger?

NEUTRALIZE

When you neutralize your mood, the selections most effective will be in the Soothing categories. A notable exception is heavy metal. You won't find heavy metal recommendations in the Soothing category, because for the majority of people, there's nothing soothing about it. But I must give credence to a great many young adults who would definitely put it there. Heavy metal legitimately soothes them, neutralizing anxiety.

For you, the Soothing category may be only the transitional music, music to initiate a swift changeover to a happier emotional and energy level. For someone else, it provides a very necessary resting place, a supportive interlude for letting go of stress and pain, perhaps the end goal itself. Again, at least a three-minute listening period is recommended.

CHANGE

When you change your mood by USEing music, your end goal is to find the music that will make you feel Soothed or Energized, whichever mood you're trying to achieve. Yes, there is a way to accomplish this, which doesn't require matching the original mood.

Conditioned Responses

Because of your conditioned responses to particular pieces of music, you may automatically reach your desired mood without first having to match your mood.

The most reachable goal for relief of physical pain is to focus on the change itself, and satiate yourself with familiar, Soothing music, music you already associate with a quietly positive state of mind. Satiate and neutralize at the same time, thus accomplishing change.

When your emotional state is the main concern, you would USE music that you already associate with a particular positive mood or activity, such as exercise, sleep, or meditation. Certain music may long have been your favorite exercise music. Hearing it gets you going, no matter what, no matter where. That is your conditioned response. Similarly, I know of a woman who had listened to opera, but had never seen one. Given a ticket as a sudden gift, she attended her first live opera performance. The opera was "La Boheme," and when the third act began, she got drowsy, fought to keep her eyes open, then went to sleep! For years, she had been using Puccini's music—especially the melodious third act—to relax before falling asleep. The music was still working, even when she didn't want it to!

That's a rather drastic example of conditioning, but it makes the point. Also, when a conditioned response is a factor, the minimum three minutes of listening to the music may be unnecessary to change your emotion. Your conditioned response to the music may switch your mood in less than one minute.

The problem remains that for everyone who achieves successful emotional crossovers with a direct move to Soothing or Energizing music, there are several more for whom it's not right. Like it or not, they need to deal with the Unsettled emotion first. Moving to the music of the desired mood or energy level first can cause irritation when your system is not ready to give up the Unsettled state without a fight, or result in only short-term improvement.

The only way to know what is right for you in this emotional analysis is to try it, after exploring the suggestions that follow. I think we are all capable of assessing what is right or wrong in our response to music. The body has an intrinsic ability to heal from within. Sometimes clearly, sometimes subtly, inner messages of "this is working" or "this is wrong" will come through. There is a wealth of self-knowledge to be gained in the upcoming pages, musicologically and psychologically. You'll find USEing music a deceptively simple system that enables you to take an immensely complex mass of material—music in all its ramifications—and activate it as a healing tool, for yourself and others.

Putting Theory into Practice:

- *Analyze the moment.* What is the mood and/or physical condition you are in now, your behavior, emotion, and physiological state?
- *Choose the correct music.* What will match the current state and what will eventually change it? Will you match an Unset-

tled mood or not? Are you working with emotional pain alone or a combination of physical and emotional pain? Does any particular music produce a conditioned response for you? If so, this would be music for emotional change, if it is Soothing or Energizing, and helpful in pain management (primarily Soothing). If not, I would suggest you find music that appeals to you within the Soothing category and condition yourself to it, to be prepared for potential confrontations with pain. What particular emotional state is your goal?

- *Determine the most appropriate sequence of music.*

> *U→S→E*
> *Unsettling → Soothing → Energizing*
> *Soothing alone*
> > *Reminder: Stimulating the Soothing emotions functions both as a transition and as a goal. Do you want to remain within the Soothing emotional space or continue on to Energizing?*
> *Soothing → Energizing*
> *Energizing alone*

Is the music chosen adequate to satiate your current state, and to achieve your desired state? Do you need to increase your listening time (more than three minutes per category), and thus the amount of music, in Unsettling, Soothing, or Energizing?

The Path to Healing

As common as any one emotion may be, we all differ in how we handle it—how, where, when, and to whom we express our feelings. These diversities occur because we have distinct, individual backgrounds of families, work histories, belief systems, and health patterns. Being mindful of this, the music selections we will be exploring are also diverse. Their unity lies in their ability to bring about specific Unsettling, Soothing, or Energizing results. Their diversity allows you to decide for yourself which selections best suit you. The diversity also provides choices in order to help others who may have no affinity for your favorite music but can be helped by another music genre. The next chapter will begin to examine healing with music as it becomes a personal journey.

2

Music Elements:

Do You
Hear What
I Hear?

EACH OF US maintains an internal Internet that determines the body's responses to all stimulants, including the elements of music. The body's physiological/neurological events are numerous and complex but we can simplify to some extent the process of music's relationship with healing. The information chip that forms the structural basis for the brain and the entire nervous system is the neuron. Neurons come in different sizes and shapes, but all are information transmitters, receiving data through one part, dendrites, and sending it out through another part, axons. Between all neurons lie gaps or synapses. When the axon part of the sender neuron is stimulated, chemical messengers are released. These are the neurotransmitters, which jump the synapses, carrying chemical information to the neuron receiver. The chemical information is turned into electrical impulse-based information, then onward to other neurons. There is considerable other chemical activity involved as well.

The entire limbic system of the brain is involved in maintaining the body's equilibrium, including emotional states. For instance, *endorphins* are peptides released in the brain that have pain-relieving effects. Think about the long-distance runner's "high"—this is an endorphin activity. Researchers are studying how music stimulates the release of these natural opiates.

The ability of a soldier to fight even after being wounded—this is *adrenal* activity. *Cortisol* is an adrenal hormone released during the "fight or flight" response to emotions, such as fear, anger, anxiety, even excitement, a "good" emotion. If anxiety (caused by, for example, stress at work, money worries, or long-term illness) is prolonged, then raised levels of cortisol may result in high blood pressure. Current research indicates that listening to appropriate music may reduce cortisol levels.

Other chemical activity includes neurotransmitters such as *norepinephrine* and *serotonin*, and low levels of either are thought to cause depression. Additionally, low levels of serotonin are being considered as a component of chronic pain. To be effective, the pain-relieving endorphins seem to require certain serotonin levels. These neurotransmitter levels may be raised by listening to the right kinds of music. When we discuss depression relief, it is possible to associate the same techniques with pain relief.

Painful muscle contractions that many people suffer as a result of anxiety, fear, or the experience of pain itself, can be alleviated by music-assisted relaxation techniques. You can see how some of the same internal conditions that cause emotional problems underlie physical pain as well and that the conditions impact, and reimpact, on each other. This is all part of the patterns of pain. All of this and more is currently the subject of intense research.

We know the crux of the processes, but not how the processes work at all levels, including the interaction of music, physical states, and emotions. The elements of music (primarily pitch, rhythm, and intensity; then melody, harmony, tempo, duration, timbre, vibrato, and texture) are transmitted as information along the neuron routes from the inner ear to the brain. This in turn activates neurotransmitters and other chemical processes in the nervous system.

My premise is that your responses to music are both causes and effects. Emotional and physical conditions → music → emotional and physical conditions. You bring something to music, music has its effect, you carry away something from music. The exact patterns will be different for us all.

Most individuals, and many age groups have their own terms for locking into the music they enjoy. A scientific term often used in music therapy is "entrainment," which encompasses both music enjoyment and music healing. The concept in music therapy of music matching mood is called the "iso-principle."[1] When you entrain to music, the music elements match what you are feeling, acting, and experiencing bodily. You with the music, the music with you. The human body seeks to entrain to music's messages in two ways, harmonically and rhythmically.

Helen Keller, both deaf and blind, learned how to dance because what remained for her, for music, was touch. She *felt* music. She could feel the dance rhythms with her feet as the floor vibrated from the music and other dancers, and she felt sound vibrations in the air.[2] Helen Keller entrained to the music's rhythmic and harmonic vibrations.

Harmonic (or resonant) entrainment involves vibrations of pitch (or frequency) and the rate of vibration per second (hertz), which stimulate brain waves. For instance, when the brain wave entrains to, or locks into, a frequency of four hertz, this induces the theta state of consciousness, which is deep relaxation, drowsiness, and light sleep.[3] Rhythmic entrainment causes locking between any two or more objects that have similar vibrating behavior. "There is an electrifying moment in the film 'The Incredible Machine' in which two individual muscle cells from the heart are seen through a microscope. Each is pulsing with its own separate rhythm. Then they move closer together. Even before they touch, there is a sudden shift in the rhythm, and they are pulsing together, perfectly synchronized."[4] The heart rate can be rhythmically entrained with music elements to advance healing. For instance, when successfully entrained, the heart will alter its rhythmic pattern to match the rhythm of music so that an irregular heart rate resumes a regular rhythm, or a resting heart rate accelerates to high-energy music.

When music changes your mood, it happens, in part, unconsciously. It is possible that the internal chemical levels which affect mood changes, are influenced by listening to music which improves certain brain responses (neuronal impulses).[5] You may end up aware of the result, the mood change, but not the beginning or midpoint of the process. Pain relief techniques working with mental imagery and music often have cleaner transitions, since the reduction in pain is more apparent than the change in the accompanying emotions. All of these areas are subjects of intense research.

Music therapists are a conduit for this technical information. There are two professional organizations, the American Association for Music Therapy and the National Association for Music Therapy, that have approved music therapy degree programs in more than seventy universities and colleges. You will find thousands of qualified music therapists throughout the world, working in rehabilitation, special education, and community settings. As health care professionals, we are very sensitive, caring musicians who specialize in the scientific application of music to achieve therapeutic results.

Helen Bonny, Ph.D., RMT/CMT, music therapist, and creator of GIM (Guided Imagery & Music), theorizes that quieting music specifically relieves pain by producing the pain-relieving peptides that effect brain responses.[6] Successful Soothing music for the guided imagery technique include George Winston's "December," "He Shall Feed His Flock," from Handel's the "Messiah," Vaughan Williams' "Rhosymedre," Villa-Lobos' "Bachianas Brasilieras No. 5," followed by Faure's "Pavane," and "Meditation" from "Thais" by Massenet.[7,8]

Psychologist and music therapist Mark Rider, Ph.D., RMT, explains that during the GIM process "a patient learns to develop a mental image of her pain—a red-hot, bubbling mass, for example—and music that matches the image (in mood, rhythm, etc.) is played. The therapist then shifts the music to a soft, soothing tone, and the patient transforms the mental image of pain into a pleasant vision—one of cool, rolling ocean waves, for instance. If the procedure is done properly, under a therapist's guidance, the patient's pain is relieved and anxiety reduced."[9]

I know music has therapeutic effect because I've used it on myself and separately have authorized a music therapy intervention study for my patients. Speaking for myself, Pachelbel's "Canon" reduces my daily stress as an oncologist. The music therapy study resulted in my cancer patients experiencing significant reductions of anxiety after two weeks of music-listening sessions.

—Philip C. McMahill, M.D.

Danielle G. suffered from deep anger and depression brought about from recently recovered memories of childhood sexual abuse. As an adjunct to counseling, it was recommended that she come to me for music therapy sessions. Additionally, we created a custom therapeutic tape in which the music goes through a variety of emotions and ends with Tchaikovsky's "Sugar Plum Fairy." The combined therapies put Danielle back on track after five months, without the need for medication.

Recently widowed, Lisa J. is a young sixty-two-year-old. "I had gone into a tailspin because my husband died suddenly. My daughter, who majored in psychology in college, told me that walking can relieve depression because chemicals are released that make it go away. So I began walking to music every day, seven days a week. The local mall has a great program for the public. Three times around equals one mile. Starting at 6 AM they pipe in all types of music—big band, Elton John, John Denver, to motivate the walkers. Walking for my health and listening to the music relaxes me, and I forget about all my problems and the problems of the world. Before I know it, I'm done—the music shortens my walking time! I feel so much better, and without medication. It works!"

> It is common knowledge that the use of exercise in the elderly is an important factor in the maintenance of health: Exercise may not add years to their lives, but it can add life to their years. . . .Exercising can be both tedious and painful, resulting in the withdrawal of many elderly from such routines. Music was found beneficial in distracting their attention and raising their threshold to pain, thereby making repetitive therapeutic movements more meaningful and acceptable to them.
>
> —Matthew H. M. Lee, M. D., MPH[10]

Bottom line: Music stimulates brain and nervous system responses that may return your body to a more healthful state, providing a drug-free therapeutic alternative for stress- or pain-related conditions. Dr. Oliver Sacks, neurologist, author of *Awakenings*, and a pianist himself, asserts that, "The power of music to integrate and cure. . .is quite fundamental," and that music serves as the "profoundest non-chemical medication" for his patients.[11]

Dr. Sacks had personal experience with therapeutic music. While climbing, he fell and shattered his leg. The rhythm in the marching or rowing songs he sang ("The Volga Boatman's Song" was one) kept his pain at bay so that he was able to make a solo descent off the mountain. In his case, favorite music rhythmically entrained him, kept his spirits up, and resulted in reduction of pain.

Let's now consider the variables inherent in music itself that make music so effective, for enjoyment and for healing. There are ten basic elements of music that remain constant throughout any and all musical styles. The balance of the elements with each other, however, is constantly in flux, sending many signals to the brain for interpretation. Great music is analogous to a great cake. The cake's ingredients combine to create a good taste. When one of the cake's ingredients is left out or overused, you do not get the taste you expect.

Similarly, the music you like includes the music ingredients you like. If you are listening to music you don't like, even if you're not consciously aware of disliking it, you will feel "out of sync" because the music's ingredients are wrong for you. When you want to match or change to a particular mood, you look for the right combination of music ingredients to make it "taste good" to you. The ten musical elements, in various combinations, at the root of your preferences for certain music, are as follows:

1. Pitch
2. Melody
3. Harmony
4. Rhythm
5. Tempo
6. Duration
7. Intensity
8. Timbre
9. Vibrato
10. Texture

1. Pitch

Pitch is the highness or lowness of a musical tone, notated as a letter: A, B, C, D, E, F, G. Pitch is determined by the frequency or rate at which sound waves vibrate per second (hertz).

Generally, the human ear can discern sounds that vibrate from 20 hertz to 20,000 hertz.[12] The pitch of an instrument depends on its length, tension, and weight. The piano's notes get deeper in pitch to the left of the keyboard and higher in pitch to the right. The violin string is shorter, tighter, and lighter, therefore higher in pitch than the bass string, which is longer, looser, and heavier. Barbra Streisand's vocal range of notes is higher than Sherrill Milnes' deep baritone voice because his vocal chords are longer than hers, creating a deeper pitch.

Pitches can be adapted to entrain emotions and physiology. "Bending" notes are pitches that change by sliding up or down to the next desired pitch. Bending notes have a sound quality that stimulates emotions such as love or sadness. Vocal and instrumental works that are in a minor key (see "Melody") will sound even more sad with bending notes; songs in a major key (also see "Melody") will feel much happier with bending notes. You'll find those notes, and those emotions, in country, folk, and blues music, for example, the country songs of k.d. lang or the bagpipes in "Amazing Grace."

Psycho-acoustic music uses patterns that replicate multiple levels of brain wave frequency patterns. This music combines pitches in such a way that states of consciousness can be altered: from beta (activity-oriented) to alpha (relaxed awareness), theta (drowsiness) or delta (deep sleep). Some of the New Age synthesized music offers prime examples, as in Dr. Jeffrey Thompson's *Isle of Skye*, which can induce alpha and theta states, or his *Egg of Time,* for inducing the delta state.

We often tend to associate high and low pitches with "good" and "bad." For instance, the music in Prokofiev's "Peter and the Wolf," describes the wolf with low-level pitches to create a foreboding character. The wolf's victim, the duck, is represented by the oboe; the bird is the flute. Opera introduces its heroes and heroines with thematic keys to their characters. Angelic harp and flute sounds are high-pitched for ethereal moods, as heard in Hilary Stagg's "Forever" from *The Edge of Forever* (new age). Low pitches can grind you into anger or, if you're in a bad mood anyway, match it. In the matching context, this music will be USEful. Via the match you could satiate the mood to work through it, then go on to neutralize and change it. Slow, low-pitched drumming can relieve tension; listen to Mickey Hart's "Mysterious Island" from *Planet Drum* (world/new age).

2. Melody

Melody is a succession of pitches up and down in a pattern. Melody is the most easily recognized and remembered of the musical elements.

Melody ranges from a short tune that asks to be hummed, sung, or whistled to the long line of notes in rock or improvised jazz. Think about the Beatles' "Yesterday," Verdi's aria "La Donna e Mobile" ("Women Are Fickle"), or W.C. Handy's "St. Louis Blues," played by Benny Goodman, then think about the long line Iron Butterfly's drummer plays during "In-A-Gadda-Da-Vida."

Melodies are made up of major and minor keys (or scales) that create specific feelings. Major keys are usually happy and cheerful, such as the "Orange Blossom Special," Mariah Carey's "Emotions," and 2 Unlimited's "Let the Beat Control Your Body," which are country, rock, and techno rock, respectively. Minor keys correspond to introspection, sadness, or a sense of mystery, for example, Chopin's "Funeral March," Garth Brooks' "The Thunder Rolls," or Counting Crow's "Perfect Blue Buildings"—classical, country and alternative rock.

A melody that descends (notes go down) for a long time may match or create a down mood, as with Tchaikovsky's "Pathetique Symphony No. 6 in B minor," in which the notes go down slowly or in "Betrayal and Desolation," from the soundtrack of "Braveheart," in which the notes descend quickly. A music line that ascends for a long time can build tension or anxiety, as in Led Zeppelin's rock noir classic "Kashmir" and the "Battle on the Ice" from Prokofiev's "Alexander Nevsky," a film score which became a classical favorite. The constant repetition of pitches within a melody line can produce a tranquil experience. You will hear this often in new age music, for example, in Jean Michel Jarre's *Equinox* or *Oxygene*, Coyote Oldman's Native American flutes and wind instruments in the meditative *Tears of the Moon*, and Mike Rowland's calming *Fairy Ring*. The absence of any stand-out melody is often preferred for concentration, which is one reason the Gregorian chant CD, *Chant*, has become such a hit.

3. Harmony

Harmony is any simultaneous combination of pitches. A three-note combination is a chord. Harmony shapes and directs melody.

When harmony joins melody, emotional depth intensifies. As melody moves through different major and minor scales, a flow of harmony is produced with successive chords. These chords can be consonant (stable) with the impression of solidity and restfulness, as in "I'd Like to Teach the World to Sing," or dissonant, giving the impression of unrest and tension. Jimi Hendrix meant to convey that in his music.

Dissonance is a major component in a lot of Unsettling music. During workshops people have told me they are nervous about listening to Unsettling music altogether, so I explain the technique of matching an adverse mood in order to deal with it directly. It helps to consider this analogy: the concept of listening to selections that produce tension, followed by music that brings about relaxation, is similar to the well-known "progressive relaxation training." This method teaches how "to tense and release various muscle groups . . . We employ tension in order to ultimately produce relaxation."[13] You can experience this same change involving dissonance and consonance by listening first to Shara Nelson's "Pain Revisited" from *What Silence Knows*, then following it with Puccini's aria "O mio babbino caro," from the opera "Gianni Schicchi."

4. Rhythm

Rhythm is the organized flow of successive pitches and rests (silences) into patterns. Rhythm propels music.

The rhythmic nature or pattern of music makes you move differently to a march or a waltz, rap, rock, country or jazz. The absolute ideal of Far Eastern rhythms deliberately lacks drive; the music asks you to be still. Cultures of India and Africa traditionally prefer irregular rhythm patterns, creating movement into tranquility or joy or a surge of energy. Gregorian chant is a smooth flow of tranquility.[14]

The heart will work to match its own rate to the rhythmic environment of music. For this reason, many people feel vaguely nervous when they hear what's called the anapestic beat. The anapestic beat is contrary to the natural heartbeat.[15] The anapestic beat pattern accents the third beat (di-di-DAH) and the heart rate accents the first beat (DAH-di). This anapestic rhythm may be the first thing that strikes you about rap. If so, think also of the stadium song "We Will Rock You." That's not rap, but it is chanted to the anapestic beat. While the anapestic beat may be disturbing or annoying to some, it's also a driving beat capable of jump-starting your energy levels.

In the rock album *House of Love*, by Christian singer Amy Grant, you'll hear anapestic rhythms that tend toward Energizing rather than Unsettled. Hip-hop music also uses anapestic beats. Even, regular rhythms that are equally Energizing are found in big band, techno, and other rock styles. Rock drummer Rod Morgenstein asserts that, "Rhythm is the most primal element in music, the driving force behind the music. On an unconscious level, it's probably the first thing people connect with, even before melody, harmony or lyrics."

5. Tempo

Tempo is the rate of speed of rhythmic recurrence: beats per minute ("bpm"), as noted in many techno rock songs.

As the pulse of music, tempo is responsible for revving you up or slowing you down—physically, emotionally, and mentally. Fast or slow tempos can change your blood pressure, heart rate, respiration, and brain wave activity. An innovative host could USE zydeco, the Cajun country music with a constant fast tempo, to revive a dull party.

One favorite USE of music is for exercise. You need to recognize that music has real power as a stimulus. If the music is too fast you may shift your balance or do a movement incorrectly and injure yourself. In the opinion of Boston sports medicine specialist Dr. Ira Grenadir, "Most athletic injuries result from simply being out of sync."[16] Criteria for faster exercise include an upbeat tempo, a melody that makes you want to sing, and rhythm without anapestic beats. Elton John's "I'm Still Standing," 2 Unlimited's techno sound in "Let the Beat Control Your Body" from *No Limits Energy*, and Nicholas Gunn's new age "Odessa" from *The Sacred Fire* meet all three criteria. Slow stretches, warm-ups, and cool downs are best suited by smooth music with predictable rhythms and slower tempos, for example, the "Largo" from the "Winter" section of Vivaldis' "The Four Seasons" and Whitney Houston's "I Have Nothing" from "The Bodyguard" soundtrack. Evenly paced phrasing is also important, which means melodic lines do not ascend or descend erratically.

Beats per minute, noted as bpm on many techno rock albums, follows a classical tradition. *Allegro* (fast), *lento* (slow), *presto* (very fast) or *largo* (very slow) are some of the tempo markings found in classical music. When you see these tempo terms on the information inserts of classical music selections, think of how you can USE them, and what activities, creative thoughts, or relaxation levels you want to achieve.

Each classical tempo comprises a range, not just one fixed number of beats, that is, *presto* has a range of 100–152 bpm.[17] A range is given rather than one speed being required, because tempo is subjective. One musician may perform the piece at *presto* 100 bpm and another musician may perform the same piece at *presto* 145 bpm. The "Lone Ranger Theme" from Rossini's "William Tell Overture" may be played very fast or sound like a tired horse! One vocalist will sing "Somewhere Over the Rainbow" slower than another singer. You may find the slower "Rainbow" emotionally heart-tugging; someone else may consider it too slow and boring.

During the 1700s, man's natural stride or walking pace was used to determine the standard tempo for most music.[18] Try walking to Vivaldi's "Largo" from "Concerto for Recorder and Orchestra" or Handel's "See the Conquering Hero Comes" and decide if this musical pace is comfortable for you. Brisker walking, for more aerobic benefit, would need faster music. The LIND (Learning In New Dimensions) Institute has recommended the tempo range of 55–70 bpm as optimal for achieving relaxed awareness (the alpha state of consciousness). Albinoni's "Adagio for Strings" falls in the Soothing range, at 60 bpm, which matches the heart at rest.

In the Energizing category, you'll find much of the music in a mid-range of 120 bpm. That's twice as fast as the "relaxed awareness" music, which stimulates you to the beta state of consciousness and includes lively activity and thinking. This tempo can bring up either Energizing or Unsettling moods. That's both the classic disco tempo and, I've been told by a former army officer, the tempo for quick time marching in the U. S. Army. You'll also find it in Unsettling "Mars, Bringer of War" from Holst's "The Planets" and Michael Frank's Energizing, jazz-based "Practice Makes Perfect." Which mood the music provokes is tempo's interaction with other elements.

6. Duration

First, duration is the basis for time and rhythm, how long a particular music element (like pitch, harmony—consonance or dissonance, rhythm, tempo, intensity or timbre) is kept up. Second, duration is the persistence of an experience, how long you listen. Consider these meanings as "inner" and "outer" duration.

The length or duration of Ravel's "Bolero," or any and all rap music, may seem interminable since there is so much repetition. "Bolero's" melody is repeated over a dozen times within sixteen minutes, with every instrument of the orchestra getting a shot at it. In the right mood, you might love it; in the wrong mood, you'll find it irritating. To a non-fan of rap, the music's rhythm and the lyrics about the day's experiences seem to go on forever, but for a rap lover, it would be a total experience.

In *Schindler's Legacy* (a book of true stories about Holocaust survivors), journalist Elinor Brecker recounted the tale of a Nazi officer who asked a violinist to play a melancholy laden Hungarian piece called "Gloomy Sunday." The violinist was a prisoner and as he played the officer's request over and over, and the officer kept drinking, the prisoner became obsessed with the idea that with this music he could kill the hated Nazi. "Gloomy Sunday's" unrelieved moroseness—its inner duration—accomplished just that. On the tenth round—its outer duration—the officer stumbled drunkenly out of the room onto the balcony and shot himself.[19]

On a happier note, Pachelbel's "Canon" was originally intended to be seven minutes long. Various interpretations range in duration as well as in use of whales, water, and instrumentation. The longest I know of is Daniel Kobialka's "Timeless Motion," which at twenty-four minutes significantly enhances relaxation. Shorter durations of listening to music may accomplish not necessarily full relaxation but a break from stress, and that may be all you want at the moment. Therefore, rather than listening to the entire piece, gradually turn the volume down. I would similarly recommend, in considering duration, that you listen to music in the Unsettling category for only a few minutes, then follow it with music from the Soothing and/or Energizing categories. You'll be trying variations of this as you work out the best method for your own stress relief.

7. Intensity

First, intensity is loudness, the volume or decibel (dB) level of the sound (deci-bel derived from 1/10th of a bel, as in Alexander Graham Bell, inventor of the telephone). Second, intensity means the degree of energy or force of the performer(s).

Decibel levels increase tenfold every 10 decibels. The alarm clock at 80dB is 100 times louder than chirping birds at 60dB. Ear damage may be sustained with prolonged listening periods at 80 decibels or more. An average rock concert registers up to 130dB. The city of Rome contracted with Pink Floyd to perform an outdoor concert at decibel levels not to exceed 60dB, out of concern for the local antiquarian ruins. Think about it: Pink Floyd at bird-chirping level!

Volume is also controlled by musicians who utilize dynamics (softer or louder) by singing or playing instruments louder (or softer) for contrast. Have you noticed how rock lovers, in particular, prefer turned-up bass? Many people of all ages have shared with me that they feel low notes within the lower areas of their bodies. Without being able to document it, I still think this response raises an interesting hypothesis.

The second definition of intensity comes into play in your reaction to the performer's degree of energy. A performer's emotional intensity can transform even the most tepid piece, but too much "drama" and it will sound fake. You will respond to additional levels of intensity in a video, and most of all, in a live concert. The interaction between audience and performer(s) has an intensity all its own. Drummer Rod Morgenstein described the experience with rock: "The audience wants to interact with the band. One of the best drum solos I've ever seen involving the audience was performed by Eric Carr of Kiss. He had the audience participate in his drum solo by having them mimic some of his drum rhythms in a kind of question and answer routine. He brought them into the solo and made them feel they were part of the show."

Nat King Cole's daughter, Natalie Cole, told me, "When I started to sing my primary goal was to make an emotional connection to the audience. I learned that from my father. I remember sitting in the audience watching his effect on people. He knew they really wanted to hear something special, they really wanted to feel. They really wanted to experience something different that he managed to give them. This was singing to your audience versus singing at them. He was so easygoing about it, so unstressed. He made each person feel that he was singing only to them."

8. Timbre

Timbre is the distinctive sound quality or "color" of tone that makes it possible for the listener to distinguish between instruments and voices.

Timbre gives the trumpet or violin a rich, bright sound and a mellow, rounded sound to the flute or clarinet. The guitars of Jimi Hendrix have extremely high decibel level squeals and electrical wrecks. The Native American flute emits trilling birdlike sounds. The pounding drums of the Japanese group Kodo sound like agile elephants. In "Tequila" the saxophone squawks "raunchy." The bright and cheery accordion dances through the zydeco tune "Jeunes Filles de la Campagne" by BeauSoleil. The upcoming section on instruments will offer more ideas.

A musician and arts administrator in his mid-40s suffered from an extreme stress condition which hit with all the symptoms of a heart attack. After he left the hospital, music therapy was recommended, but he found that for him only a certain kind of music was really effective for releasing tension. This music had certain timbres—the low sustained notes of woodwinds and strings, balanced with nature sounds of birds and babbling brooks. "I listened to it mostly in the car because I was driving a lot at that time. The music's effect was very relaxing, helping to dissipate the stress in my life. Also I think it worked the best because it was almost subliminal. I didn't feel it necessary to interpret form and analysis as I usually would do with classical or country music."

Many classical musicians also prefer to listen to minimalist music for relaxation. This is music that is nonjarring, nonenergizing, and lacking melody or noticeable timbres. This combination of music elements usually found in the new age style is particularly soothing, not demanding attention.

9. Vibrato

Vibrato is a periodic change in frequency, heard as an extended or slight tremor effect.

Singers vary in this warbling effect of their voice. Opera singers use it to great dramatic effect, since operas tell a story. Think too about the difference in vibrato between female vocalists Whitney Houston, Dolly Parton, Da Brat, and Toni Braxton. Or the vibrato variations of Rod Stewart, Elvis Presley, and B. B. King. The organ can produce a range of vibrato speeds, whereas the piano cannot. The string player shakes the left hand at a steady fast or slow rate of speed. The effect? The rate of vibrating speed or lack of any vibrato creates emotions ranging from exciting and vibrant to blah and depressed. Listen to the fast vibrato of gospel organ, which fills your heart, compared to the synthesized organ of rap, which keeps the vibrato out, not allowing the listener to feel love, joy, or optimism.

10. Texture

Texture is the pattern of music created by quantity of tones or lines played or sung together. Think of it as the thickness or thinness of the music.

When a single instrument or voice plays or sings a melody, the one voice is called "monophonic." It has a thin texture. "Polyphony" occurs when two or more voices or instruments play separate lines, making it a thicker texture. A composition for a string quartet will be thinner than the same piece arranged for full orchestra. The Gregorian chants of Chanticleer's "Missa Mater Patris" have a polyphonic texture and are thicker than the Gregorian chants of the Benedictine Monks of Santo Domingo de Silos, which are sung in unison. Both may relax you. A full concert choir singing the "Hallelujah Chorus" from Handel's "Messiah" is thicker than both—and Energizing.

Texture is frequently involved when "focus" becomes important to you. A large group that produces a thick texture may keep the focus outside yourself—useful for getting ready for work or school. A full band playing Sousa's "Stars and Stripes Forever" could do the trick, as well as the big band instrumental "Chattanooga Choo-Choo" or Elton John's Rock song "I'm Still Standing." A single instrument may be the best aid to concentration and inner centering, for meditation or sleep. Many authors have told me that they use all sorts of music as background "to filter out the world," but that for actual writing a single instrument proves the most effective. Christopher Parkenings' guitar music is often recommended as are Galway's flute solos. You might also like "Liebestraum (Love Dream) No. 3," which Liszt composed for solo piano.

Lyrics

The correlation of music and lyrics is important. Thus, I have included it as an eleventh element, not a constant in all music, but a vital component when present. The pros and cons of rock lyrics are not the point of discussion, rather, I am interested in lyrics' relevance to healing.

When lyrics and music go hand in hand, they give each other power, they communicate the same message. Even the greatest words will be lost if the music is not good. The best music will give more meaning to the lyrics. If the music does not match the words, then the "message" can be confusing. Listen to rhythm & blues group Smokey Robinson and the Miracle's "The Tears of a Clown"; the music is lighthearted, while the lyrics are sad. In many cases, this is what the composer/lyricist wanted—it gets your attention. For accomplishing what you need in a healing program, however, it's simply more effective if the music and words match the same mood.

Several years ago, producer Aaron Spelling ("The Love Boat," "Melrose Place") had an idea for a new television series called "Finder of Lost Loves." An admirer of Burt Bacharach's songs, he commissioned Burt and Carole Bayer Sager to write the theme for the new series. They came up with a beautiful melody, and the next question was who was going to sing the title song.

"Aaron Spelling had the idea to ask Dionne Warwick," Burt said. "The more I thought about the song, the more I agreed how perfect Dionne would be to sing it."

This was 1985 and Burt and Dionne had not worked together in years. Their earlier collaborations, along with Hal David, had scored an incredible thirty-nine consecutive Top Ten hits, but a rift had developed and split up the team. All three had moved on to new writing and recording partners, each with their own successes. They had not spoken to each other for ten years.

Burt did not know how Dionne would respond to hearing from him, but decided it was worth a try. He called, and they set a time for him to go to Dionne's house so he could play her the song. "I was so nervous," Dionne recalls. "It was like waiting for a blind date." Burt said that when he got there he headed straight for the piano—"the most comfortable place for me in times of stress." Both he and Dionne agree that what happened was magic. "After seven bars, I realized Dionne was singing the lyrics that would bring us back together:

Put your past behind you,
Leave your heart open.

"No one has ever sung my music the way Dionne does. I've always known that, and I stopped and told her. It was as though the problems of the past few years had disappeared."

"Finder of Lost Loves" was not a long-running series, but Dionne and Burt's reunion has been. They have been touring in performances together now for ten years.

Country music has always been famous for "somebody done somebody wrong songs" and the expert wordplay in new country is one of its strongest points. We'll look further at the mutual strength in music and lyrics in the styles section, not only for country, but for folk, blues, gospel, soul, and Christian.

Instruments

As I mentioned earlier, certain instruments and configurations of instruments also produce varying feelings and aspects of healing, due to their timbres or "colors." This is another dimension to consider in your healing program.

Strings include the violin, viola, cello, and bass, plus their instrumental "cousins," such as the acoustic guitar, mandolin, harp, Indian sitar and tambura, zither, Chinese erhu, Yugoslavian gusle, banjo, African lute, Swedish dulcimer, the Baroque viola de gamba or Japanese koto. The general nature of strings is to soothe and bring feelings of soaring peace and harmony. Scoring that is too heavy for strings can cause tension and simulate terror. Hitchcock knew that and composer Bernard Herrmann gave him the sound he wanted in many movies. Remember the shower scene in "Psycho"?

Woodwinds include flute, piccolo, oboe, English horn, clarinet, bassoon, soprano, alto, tenor, and "bari" saxophones, plus their "cousins," such as the harmonica (mouth organ), Chinese sheng, Spanish tiple, Indian shehnai, South American panpipes, Japanese shakuhachi, and ocarina. This group of instruments produces predominantly airy, transparent feelings—lightness, clarity, and delicate grace. But a composer can heighten that. Think about the clarinet's bright sensuality that opens Gershwin's "Rhapsody in Blue," the lonely, elegant English horn in Sibelius' "Swan of Tuonela," the heavenly flute of James Galway playing "Song of the Seashore," or the heart-tugging saxophone of Kenny G in *Breathless*.

Brass includes the French horn, trumpet, trombone, and tuba, plus related instruments such as the Scandanavian lur, Swiss alphorn, and Australian didgeridoo. The effect of brass can be Energizing, as with Wagner's "Overture to Die Meistersinger," or a German oompah band. Muted brass becomes haunting and mysterious in Ravel's Soothing "Pavane pour une infante defunte," while heavy brass can produce Unsettled feelings of irritability, even terror. Listen to two classical works, "Toccata" and "Fanfare" from Karl Husa's "Music for Prague 1968" or Janacek's "Sinfonietta" to hear this effect.

Percussion can be electronic or acoustic and even organic, if body parts are played. Drums from around the world include the bass, snare, tympani, udu, tablas, hoop, congas, djembe, dundun, gudugudu, and Caribbean steel drum. Other percussion instruments include cymbals, marimba, xylophone, chimes, bells, water phone, Native American rattles, and Tibetan singing bowls—and the pots and pans that a one-year-old pounds.

Since percussion affects the body's normal rhythms, primarily the heart rate and respiration, it is often used in the healing ceremonies of several cultures, including Native American and African. Taken to the extreme, drumming voodoo-style in distinctly nonhealing ceremonies is intended to induce orgies, inflict harm, and even cause death.[20] More positively, Mickey Hart's *Planet Drum* is a celebration of eclectic percussion sounds. Tony Wells' *Weatherspace* is an ethereal new age compilation of thunderstorm, rain, and wind effects, combined with flutes, chimes, waterphones, gongs, bells, ting chas (small cymbal-like bells), and dun chen (Tibetan trumpet). The effect is very Soothing.

The voice is also considered an instrument, in terms of music elements. Frank Sinatra and Ella Fitzgerald pull all the hurt-by-life pain strings. The Nylons, pop vocalist Bobby McFerrin, and the gospel group Sweet Honey in the Rock, are examples of strong voices singing a cappella (without instrumental backup), which can provide music for your healing program. A music therapy technique that I often employ during workshops is called "Name That Tune."[21] When "The Flight of the Bumblebee" is played, featuring Yo-Yo Ma on cello and singer Bobby McFerrin, almost everyone has trouble identifying both instruments; they can hear "a stringed instrument," but rarely do they catch the singer's voice intertwined with the cello.

Your Educated Ear

"I teach music appreciation to nonmusic students. They can't hear what I hear, because it is a long journey to liberate the ear. I understand, because musicians are luckier. Playing an instrument or singing infuses life into music—like CPR—and you hear it in a richer dimension." This was the analysis of composer Milton Schafer whose "He Touched Me" is a Barbra Streisand classic.

The Sound of Healing is a bit like taking a simplified music appreciation course, in that the reasons for "liberating the ear" involve finding the healing components of music. You don't have to "know music" to do this. You do have to understand what music can mean.

I know of many people, young and old, male and female, who are tone-deaf, but their enjoyment of music is full tilt. Their lives are filled with music that *means* something to them. One such man hears the first few notes of a popular song and can tell you the title, who performed it, and when. He "liberated his ear" to include a lot of classical and new age music that effectively calms him down or revs him up. His eight-year-old daughter, also tone-deaf, constantly sings her heart out, not hitting all the right notes, but totally expressing her feelings, just like her dad.

Tone-deaf or acutely sensitive, you'll still be able to analyze music for its health-effectiveness. To illustrate, let's examine rocker Peter Gabriel's "Mercy Street" from *So* and Mark O'Connor's country instrumental, the "Orange Blossom Special" from *The New Nashville Cats.*

When you listen to a song or an instrumental work, there are certain elements that most people hear first. The first thing I diagnose is the tempo—is it fast, slow, or medium? Peter Gabriel begins "Mercy Street" with low organ sounds that slide around with only an occasional drum beat that lacks tempo or rhythm. This immediately makes me feel Unsettled. Then the repetitious rhythm kicks in with lonely bell sounds played at a medium-fast pace, arousing emotions of worry and unease. The drums join the dismal repetition with a different rhythm at the same medium tempo. Then Peter's voice enters with a ghostlike quality, singing lyrics that speak of dark loneliness and lost dreams. His message is depressingly metaphoric. I can't figure out exactly what happens. The thin texture of only a few instruments whose timbres lack luster makes the music hit my inner core of discomfort. The synthesizer imitates the vocal melody with lack of vibrato, sounding dull and lifeless. This song is definitely depressing me as the final words come in, ". . .looking for mercy. . ." I'll remember this selection when I'm really "in the mood" to match it.

The "Orange Blossom Special," however, is very fast and immediately picks me up. This is fine, because I'm ready to stop being depressed. In fact, the tempo takes off and never slows down in Mark O'Connor's version. This could, depending on my mood at another time, irritate me because I don't want to speed up. However, I want to mood match now, after hearing "Mercy Street," and go with the tempo. I don't need a transition piece, because I'm so familiar with this technique. Another time, though, I might need the emotional space of Soothing music.

The rhythm is very steady and regular, which makes it easier for me to get "in step." Now there's pitch. The rhythm section is playing lower and the fiddle is all over the place, high and low, changing fast, holding my interest. The harmonies are pleasing, balanced with a bit of dissonance. I hear bending notes—just a little bit of emotional attachment creating that happy state. O'Connor's band has a thicker texture (several instruments which sound very "full") that would be good for focusing outside of myself. The duration of the piece is longer than most versions because of short bursts of other recognizable melodies (including the theme from "The Flintstones," which makes me laugh) he tosses in. The entire band never lets up in its intensity, and the combination of timbres from all of the various instruments makes the sound really Energizing. Vibrato? Everybody's playing too fast to really hear any. I'd definitely place this music on my Energizing list, for driving and for a fast start after getting out of bed in the morning.

Begin observing what it is that you like about various pieces of music. What you don't like may readily appear as a red flag. Or you may develop a slow discomfort for a piece, although you may not be aware of it immediately. Do some musical detective work to find out what sounds wrong. The more specific you can be about what musical elements you don't and do like, the more music you can bring into your healing program.

3

You and Your Music:
Collection
Analysis

ALL OF US feel a variety of emotions, from boredom to anger to grief to love. To match your moods effectively, it's important that your music library reflect a broad range of emotions. Then, given a variety of activities throughout the day, your music library should also incorporate music you like to hear when eating, exercising, driving, reading, staring at screens (television or computer), and creating dinner for six in a half hour—all that your days, manic or mild, consist of.

Start with organizing your collection into a classification system that works for you. Memory aids are also useful, for organizational follow-up, so two possibilities are suggested below. USE whatever technique is appropriate for your schedule and for what you individually need to accomplish, keeping in mind the dual goals: identification of music choices with health benefits, and ease of access to your selections.

Classifications

By music style. This is what most of us do. The descriptions of musical styles and their substyles in the next three chapters will help you further systematize an unwieldy or haphazard "rock" or "easy listening" section. Classical music lovers tend to organize their collections by composer, form, and/or instrument. For other styles of music, organization by performer, single or group, is more common. If you have a conglomeration that you mentally term "other," the sixteen music styles listed and described in chapters 4, 5, and 6 will serve as guidelines for bringing order out of "other" chaos.

By activity. If you're constantly on the go, it might be easier for you to organize your music collection by the kind of activity you want the music to accompany. You might label your collection of CDs and/or tapes "Relaxing," "Studying," "Driving," or "Exercising."

Either classification method could be supplemented, and further developed, by memory aids, two of which would be especially helpful in your music healing program.

USE color-coded dots. Classify each CD or tape into a USE category by placing a colored dot on the visible edge—for example, navy blue for *Unsettling;* green for *Soothing;* and red for *Energizing.* Many of your tapes and CDs will contain multi-USE music; this is especially true for soundtracks and stage show scores. Color coding track lists would be valuable as well. The next technique will help you accomplish this and, in general, make your collection more organized.

Make notes. As you pull out a selection to listen to, note at least two items of information, either on the insert or in a separate file or notebook. Note the Unsettling/Soothing/Energizing emotional range you connect with that piece of music; an activity the music has successfully accompanied; the length of the piece; and, finally, your perception of the tempo.

S(low) would be about one beat per second (60 beats per minute);

M(edium) would be walking pace (70–100 beats per minute);

F(ast) would be your comfort zone for running or fast exercising (100+ beats per minute).

Sample notes might then read: *E/making dinner/5 min. /M* or *S/reading/12 min. /S.*

You could continue to identify each piece by an emotion with which the music correlates. This would require you to focus your attention on each piece and may necessitate your listening to each piece more than once. It is easier, and faster, and *not wrong* to make a basic assessment, for example, of "relaxation and peace," or "happy and optimistic." Emotions are fluid; sorrow relates to melancholy, as joy relates to excitement. Being as specific as possible when assessing your emotions is fine, but don't go overboard. As the Nike promotion dictum states, "Just do it." Identify your emotions by whatever first comes to mind.

As a result of your coding and note taking, you will be able to quickly find your targeted health maintenance music selections and identify a moderate range of emotions to which they relate. A secondary benefit, at least from a health program perspective, will be the wheat-from-chaff separation. Don't consign a CD or tape to the trash can because only two of twelve tracks have entertainment value or health resource potential. Many music lovers record the lone selections they like on separate tapes. Similarly, you could incorporate the selection that has mood-matching benefit into activity-related or personalized USE tapes. Then find a CD/tape exchange store.

Specialized Tapes

I encourage making special tapes for personal use, but realize your ambition depends on the amount of time you can give to the project. Whether you make separate mood-matching or activity-related tapes is your choice. There are no "musts" with this, only options.

UNSETTLING/SOOTHING/ENERGIZING TAPES

Working with your insert notations, compile three tapes, one each of All-Unsettling, All-Soothing, and All-Energizing. By interchanging these tapes, you can listen to whatever mood-matched music you need, in the sequence you need. The All-Soothing tape could prove especially valuable in creating conditioned responses to music for USE in pain management.

A fourth tape, one of specific emotions sequenced through the three USE categories, is possible. However, that would be more appropriately done by working with a qualified music therapist, one who is able to work with you and assess not only the type of music you need but the duration that each category should be given.

Unsettling

Some emotions you could assign to your music as *Unsettling*: sadness, mournfulness, grief; depression (see caution that follows), melancholiness, gloom; anxiety, fear, restlessness; agitation, anger, agony.

Unsettling music is intended for working through a mood you're already in, so be careful how long you listen to a selection in this category. Pain sufferers may find that Unsettling music is helpful in attacking their emotions involved with pain, but they will be better served in obtaining specific pain relief by choosing Soothing music, which evokes Soothing imagery. (Music that evokes such images is described in chapter 9, beginning on p. 125. We'll also discuss other Soothing choices which may work for you. If appropriate, when you're ready, continue on to Energizing choices.)

When working with Unsettling music, the appropriate duration for changing the emotional state will vary with each individual, but, in general, the longest listening time I recommend is seven minutes, with three minutes being the minimal time for effectiveness.

Caution: If you are experiencing clinical depression, utilize professional counseling through the aid of a qualified music therapist, to help you explore the realm of healing music.

Soothing

Moods and emotions considered *Soothing* are: tenderness, sentimentality, love; calmness, peacefulness, contentment; tranquility, serenity, detachment; relaxation, meditation, reverence.

Energizing

Emotions you might assign to your music as *Energizing* are: lightheartedness, gaiety, playfulness; cheerfulness, merriment, happiness; joy, optimism, robustness; enthusiasm, excitement, exhilaration.

ACTIVITY TAPE

In the basic method for making an activity tape, your sorting notes continue to be your reference. Generally, the length of time required or allocated to accomplish the activity must first be determined, so your tape is the correct length. Next, choose the music that matches the activity, either by the emotions that accompany it, and/or the speed (tempo) at which you go about it. Then, decide the sequence in which you want the various pieces to play. Finally, record the mix.

EXERCISE TAPE

What is your favorite exercise routine and how long do you do it? For example, a five-minute warm-up might best match one or two medium-tempo songs; alternatively, you could extend your warm-up to the length of the songs. (Don't skimp on the warm-up; it's important to get your muscles loosened before going on to more intensive exercise. Music can help you allow adequate time for this.) Next, the aerobic section would use fast-tempo music for twenty to thirty minutes. The ten-minute cooldown USEs slow-tempo music, and a single music selection could last the full ten minutes. The resultant tape is thirty-five to forty-five minutes, one side of a ninety-minute tape. (Refer to "Tempo" in chapter 2 for specific exercise music ideas.)

SLEEP TAPE

Do you have trouble falling asleep at night? Take a moment to think about what general mood you are in when you go to bed. Frequently, a sleep-preventing emotion, or mix of emotions, is in the Unsettling or Energizing groups, as will be the correlated music. Choose one to three of those emotions and match the music to them.

Three minutes is the recommended minimum time for the first part of the sleep tape, with a maximum of fifteen minutes. Then sequence to the music that will Soothe you into sleep, approximately two times the length of the first section. That would give you a tape between nine and forty-five minutes in length (Unsettling/Energizing: three–fifteen; Soothing: six–thirty). Jeffrey Thompson's *Isle of Skye* (new age), Hilary Skagg's "Forever" (new age) Jean Michel Jarre's *Equinox* (new age), Autechre's "Windwind" (trance rock) and Mickey Hart's "Mysterious Island" (world) are five good Soothing choices.

If you are truly exhausted, the Unsettling music may not be needed; Soothing music alone could bring on sleep. If you are tranquil and relaxed already, you'll probably not need any music, but listening to the Soothing group would pleasurably enhance the calm, drowsy feeling.

WAKE-UP TAPE

Is your alarm clock too jarring or is the radio playing the wrong music at 6:10 AM? Overly energetic music will disorient you when you awake; music that is too soft will make you dawdle and drift. A special wake-up tape could start your day positively.

Begin with at least three minutes of the Soothing music that put you to sleep the night before. Then, if you like and your morning schedule allows, add another Soothing piece, such as Vaughan Williams' "The Lark Ascending" (classical). Sequence next to Energizing, preferably choosing a piece that starts out slowly, for example, the "William Tell Overture" (classical), Yanni's "Swept Away" (new age), or Michael Franks' "Practice Makes Perfect" (jazz), so you don't hit the ceiling with trumpets blaring! To keep the momentum going, either have another Energizing tape available, or add more favorites to this tape.

DRIVING TAPE

A special driving tape can help you control your moods, enhancing your ability to make safe driving decisions. Anger and frustration are the bane of many drivers. Music also will help override boredom, which is not an emotion per se, but is a dangerous condition to be in when you're at the wheel.

Record your favorite songs, categorized by Energizing fast tempos for side "A," to keep you awake, and Soothing slow-tempo music on side "B," to calm your anger or frustration. Automobile tape and CD decks now have the capability to switch directly from one track to another, from side to side easily. You might also make specific Energizing and/or Soothing tapes (coded as "E" or "S") for each favorite music style, for example, rock/E, rock/S, classical/E, classical/S, country/E, country/S, etc., which would be welcome for longer drives and to add variety to weekly commutes.

Possible music selections for special activity tapes are suggested in chapters 7 through 10 and in Appendix A and B. Consider these as supplements to the music you already know you like and have found effective in similar circumstances. By the way, if you are sharing listening space with another person, I recommend you either agree on music selections or wear headphones to decrease potential mayhem inside the car, house, office, or neighborhood.

Reminder: Neither the reorganization of your collection or making specialized tapes for personal use need to be done all at once, nor is your final accumulation a fixed entity. People change, as does the response to, and need for, certain music changes.

Your Music and You

As you go about the reorganization process, take time to consider what your collection says about you:

- What did you once love, now dislike, or find boring?
- Why don't you like this work/song/performer anymore?
- What do you think this says about you? No judgment allowed, only healthy curiosity.
- Have you grown? Are you deeper, gentler, more sophisticated, more open to new things, or more in a rut?
- In your own analysis, does your music collection validate the person you are now?
- Are you instinctively turning to certain favorites at certain times?
- Is your collection mostly new age-mellow or is it primarily devoted to cheerful, upbeat music? Are you specializing in dissonance?
- Do you have a variety of styles?

These last six queries in particular are important within the framework of your music healing program. To make your collection beneficial as a health resource, you will need, in addition to the favorites you already turn to, a full complement of Unsettling, Soothing, and Energizing choices—including some of, but certainly not limited to, the recommended works. Assess possible activities, the reality of your emotional life, and your need for pain management. Then decide where your collection needs some filling-in-the-holes.

Extending Your Collection

At this point, some suggestions on savvy music shopping are in order. The USE selections in chapters 7 through 10 have been carefully thought out, and I have no hesitation in advising that these would be good additions to your collection. You might want to be just a bit wary in accepting friends' recommendations as absolutes, however. The following questions are a good check:

Does my friend have the same taste in music I do?
What aspect of the music or the performance was so appealing?
Was my friend involved in any particular activity at the time?
Is his/her enthusiasm for an entire tape/CD, or only one part of it?

A relevant story is in order here:

After a miscarriage and all of its emotional trauma, Carrie A. reluctantly attended a baby shower. She would have been eight months' pregnant, as was the mother-to-be, but Carrie had miscarried. The room was full of loving friends and the music "Enigma" was so soothing that she broke down in tears. Eventually, Carrie ended up as an exhausted but creative guest; together, they all made a baby quilt. Carrie considered the whole experience of combining music and artistic effort great therapy. Some time later, for a relaxing moment at work, Carrie's husband was playing "Enigma" in his office and a coworker became visibly restless and abruptly left the room. He later explained, a little sheepishly, that this was the music he and his wife listened to while making love.

A number of people have told me they also like "Enigma"— not for relaxing, emotional catharsis, or quilts, but for great sex! Therefore, thank your friends for their recommendations, and continue to do what you can to determine your own, uninfluenced reaction. You might also give a second chance to music you're not sure of, listening to it again when you are in a different mood or involved in a different activity.

RADIO

One of the best ways to shop for different music styles is via your radio. The unfortunate part of "radio shopping" occurs when you hear a terrific piece—but the name is not given. In stores or at a friend's house, you would not hesitate to ask what's playing. That is possible with a radio station too. Note the specific time you heard the selection and the call letters of the station. Check the telephone directory, call the station, and ask for program information.

VIDEO

Being able to see your favorite artist(s) perform is a terrific step up from hearing a recording. The energy and intensity of a great video-taped concert or a visual montage and storyline interpreting your current favorite CD track gives new dimension to the music and gives you a whole new way of appreciating a performer's talent.

MUSIC STORE

The ideal store will have:

- A wide variety of CDs and tapes
- Listening booths
- Salespeople who are familiar with more than one kind of music

My favorite store has the ambience of a large department store: high ceilings, decorator colors, and well-thought-out merchandise displays. Look for a store that has a depth of selection in all music styles, a savvy sales staff, and many listening booths. High ceilings and lots of room make you feel more comfortable—room to breathe, browse, and feel the music. The music playing overhead should switch in styles and tempos, from vocal to instrumental, to meet the listening needs of a variety of store patrons. Either that, or each music category should have its own separate enclosed area, where that music is played.

Listening stations are the single most important service a store can provide. Sadly, many urban stores opt not to have them, citing lack of space. Listening booths were common just a few decades ago and are making a comeback, but I would like to see them required in all music stores. (Back in the "really old" days, when records were not as common as sheet music, stores provided a piano player to help customers choose selections. Interestingly, that was one of George Gershwin's first jobs.) If your store has a limited selection of styles, it may indicate that local demographics, which drive management's purchasing decisions, focus on classical, Christian, country, jazz, R & B, or new age. Start requesting what you want.

Crossing Over and Future Fusion

The knowledgeability of the sales staff takes on added weight when you consider not only the number of performers found in

any one style but the prevalence of stylistic crossovers and fusion.
Will you buy Elton John's music in the popular or rock category? Beastie Boys were found in the punk rock section, then rap, and now in classic blues with hip-hop. B. B. King is known as the "King of Blues and Soul," but you can also find him in the gospel, jazz, and R & B categories. Amy Grant's music is placed in both the Christian and rock sections. James Galway's music is found in classical, folk, new age, and easy listening. Pat Metheny can be found in jazz and new age. Eric Clapton is considered a blues and rock performer. Hami does rap and a hip-hop version of classical. Ralph Stanley is found in bluegrass and now gospel, with Joe Isaacs. Mark O'Connor plays country, blues, jazz, world, and now classical, with the Concordia Orchestra.

Recording companies and music stores experience constant frustrations trying to categorize music, because the personal creativity of artists today breeds crossovers. This mélange of styles actually enriches both the industry and its audience—you, the listener. A recent letter in *Billboard* (the music industry's newspaper) concerned rock but, by extension, holds true for many styles and many music lovers:

> *Listeners do not want to be put in boxes. The massive success of Hootie and the Blowfish, Collective Soul, and 'Encomium: A Tribute to Led Zeppelin' all attest to the rock audience demanding music it wants to hear. . .across all formats. Rock listeners have broader tastes than niche formats. . .for the simple reason they liked the song. . ."*
> —Danny Buch, V. P. Promotion, Atlantic Records, New York[1]

In order to achieve a "user-friendly" format for this book, music styles are discussed within two frameworks:

1. The music style categorizations you would find in most music stores (chapters 4, 5, and 6).
2. The mood-matching correlation of music to emotion (chapters 7 through 10, and Appendix A and B).

If you are dejectedly facing a collection with a lot of holes, or one with just enough holes to be annoying, this format is geared to help you decide which new material to add to your collection, and understand why you need it.

One new fusion factor borders on "con-fusion" and is fast approaching with technology. Among the high-tech forerunners is rock artist Todd Rundgren. He believes that while most people just want music "to start and end by itself," a CD-ROM user "at any particular time, can hijack the train." Rundgren was referring to the CD-ROM software he has developed, "No World Order," which "lets the listener adjust the mood, tempo, and other features of an album."[2] A number of technology firms are experimenting with this concept and CD enhancement, and it is fascinating. Sooner rather than later, we may all feel free to change whatever we don't like in any piece of music. Will we be considered lazy or purist if we just want the music to play through till the end? I don't know. Roll over, Beethoven!

Until then, enjoy the personal challenge in this chapter, and enjoy the benefits and sheer listening pleasure that result. Given the versatility of music and the constant shifting of your activities, state of health, and emotions, all music has the potential to be therapeutic as well as enjoyable.

You'll always be sure of your favorite style. You like what you like. Based on that, there's a probability that you will gravitate first to one or a few of the music styles, so skip now, if you wish, to the style that most appeals to you. Within that segment, you will discover what other music styles are recommended because they relate directly to what you already prefer. My hope is that you'll become intrigued and eventually investigate all the styles. As you read this book, you will be examining each style's predominant audio effects and healing capabilities, as well as what makes each one unique and similar to others. You might find the unique aspects fairly recognizable. I think some of the similarities will surprise you.

Music exalts each joy, allays each grief, expels diseases, softens every pain, subdues the rage of poison and the plague.

—John Armstrong, M. D. *The Art of Preserving Health,* 1744.

The Wide
World
of Music:

ALL THINGS CONSIDERED

4

Wisdom of the Heart:

Blues/
Gospel/Soul/
Folk/Country/
Christian

THE STYLES IN this chapter have a common thread—that of being music of the heart more than music of the mind. Of course, there is heart-touching music in all styles, yet somehow that special meaning is exemplified in blues, gospel, soul, folk, country and Christian music. Among the emotions you are likely to find are love, sadness, reverence, and joy. If you are not already familiar with these styles, there is a deep well of love and sharing of life's problems herein.

If you are feeling sad, lonely, grief-stricken, or melancholy, songs in any of the above music styles might prove to be just the right medium of healing for you. The more intensely you connect with the music, the greater the possibility of pulling out of your deepest self the feelings that are keeping you Unsettled.

You will find that certain songs in country or Christian music songs will be key Soothing music choices for you. For tapping into Energizing emotions and accelerating physical energy, there is a bounty of material. With the rhythms of gospel and Christian music, some muscles will demand to move, while the words remind you that God brought love into the world. Soul and country music encompass moods from doleful to "let's dance," and you'll find renewed energy levels in the livelier songs. The only exception I would make here concerns loneliness and the blues. The blues are highly effective for matching the Unsettled mood of loneliness, and they may or may not soothe or energize you out of your mood. Loneliness is the heart of the blues.

Blues

Blues music involves call-response patterns and bending notes, creating cries of depression, pain, and sorrow.

Understanding how the blues came into being will give you an added perspective on its role as one of your new musical possibilities. In the United States, during the 1800s, the impoverished black country people sang about life's troubles. "Nobody Knows the Trouble I've Seen" was real life talking. Those slow, mournful melodies found their way into the streets of New Orleans, becoming the street cries of peddlers selling their wares. Rhythm is not the essential element, rather it is the intensity of emotion that is crucial to the blues heartfelt fervor. That fervor has kept the blues alive. Blues has more than historical meaning; it's still vital. A recent blues festival in Chicago drew 100,000 people in one weekend, in the rain.

The natural way in which emotions are communicated through the blues is very powerful, using the call-response pattern to make it easy for listeners to get involved. "Call-response" patterns feature the solo instrument or voice "calling" to other instruments who answer or "respond." blues music is usually found in the Unsettling category because it talks about life's troubles and acknowledges pain and sorrow, specifically loneliness, as realities of life. Bill Shahrooz, a blues guitar player and occupational therapist, commented, "The blues historically were known as the 'devil's music'; music for sinning. I think music about sinning and being sinned against is more to the point."

You would choose blues music to accomplish a cathartic release of underlying troubled feelings. Voices of the past are found in classic blues recordings. Current examples include Bonnie Raitt's "The Road's My Middle Name" and Eric Clapton's "Tore Down."

Bill Shahrooz offers a personal insight: "If I've had a fight with my wife just before leaving for a gig or, if I feel scattered just trying to get to the gig, these negative feelings are the best catalyst for improvising blues passionately. The worst playing situation would be feeling no emotion, just blah." Bill finds that when the Unsettled emotion he is feeling is matched with the music he performs, then "once I'm there and playing the blues I'm transformed. I'm then ready to deal with problems because I feel renewed."

Singer Natalie Cole agrees with Bill. "We just did some blues in Los Angeles and I came off stage feeling so great! Some great old blues stuff: Etta James and Joe Walsh. Blues is like a good cry, exactly. I know that night there were people who were boo-hooing and afterwards they felt so good. Isn't that interesting how blues can do that to you? Sometimes I even get caught up in it and I get emotional."

The genre greats like B. B. King, Bessie Smith, Billie Holiday, and T. Bone Walker were eulogized and their special blues sound was incorporated into soul, jazz, classical, and folk music. Folk singer Joni Mitchell sang the blues in the mid-60s. Michael Bolton has been called the "blue-eyed soul or white boy singing the blues."[1] Guitarist Eric Clapton went from classic rock to blues and ballads and created blends of all three. The deep blues sound of Junior Kimbrough's "Lord, Have Mercy on Me" from *Sad Days, Lonely Nights* is very similar to the Rolling Stone's *Sticky Fingers* and *Exile on Main Street* (the group named themselves after Muddy Waters' great blues song). Bill Shahrooz recommended, "Upbeat blues such as the boogie and shuffle, for example, 'Let the Good Times Roll' and ZZ Top's 'La Grange.'"

If the blues is already a favorite, you'll also find the melancholy blues sound in the "Second Movement" of Ravel's "Sonata for Violin and Piano" and in Josh White Jr./Robin Batteau's "House of the Rising Sun." Sade's song, "Pearls," might be just the right pick for you. If you really connect with the thin textures and mournful emotions that "Pearls" communicates, you might also try these prime Unsettling examples: Peter Gabriel's "Mercy Street," k.d. lang's "Outside Myself" or Chopin's "Funeral March." All five are detailed in chapter 8 and Appendix A.

Gospel

Gospel music employs God-centered lyrics that make the spirit soar with an energetic repetition of call-response.

Gospel music originated with the work songs of southern black laborers, songs that would relieve monotony and inspire weary bodies to keep going. These work songs developed into spirituals, sung with great rhythmic fervor. The great artists Reverend James Cleveland and Mahalia Jackson rode the wave of popularity that started in the 1940s and climaxed in the 1960s, both being mentors for Aretha Franklin. In 1952, gospel music was called "a revival of 'stunt evangelism,'" but even critics had to admit that gospel made the sung praise of the Lord as "familiar to the people as the tunes crooned by Bing Crosby."[2] In black communities, gospel singing was a way of life, in the churches, road shows and revivals. Then audiences wanted gospel music in folk fests and symphony halls as well.

When gospel took to the road, "Rock Me" and "Nearer to Thee" traveled the country. As singers bumped into one another, gospel mixed with blues and jazz. "From this kind of vibrant dialogue, black American music has grown, a call-and-response between the plain truths of clean, rural forms and the complex sophistication of new lives, new sounds in the city."[3]

For you, the rhythms of gospel may provide the musical spiritual uplift to change your state from one of melancholy to rhythmic energy. Any blues song can be imbued with gospel fervor by changing the lyrics (from "these are my troubles" to "let God handle your troubles"), adding more singers, speeding up the tempo, and starting the energetic 1-2-3-4 rhythm. Natalie Cole, who recently included a black gospel choir in her Las Vegas shows, demonstrated in her show that even the most jaded audience is moved to tap their toes, swing their heads, clap hands, and half-stand/half-sit in their chairs.

Shirley Caesar has continued the gospel tradition of a strong woman with a strong voice. Sweet Honey in the Rock is a female gospel group. An anthropologist who appreciates the life energy of gospel music said of them, "What a sound! Pure a cappella and pure strength. Their sense of power as women, black women, is in every note." Aretha Franklin, whose father was a minister in Detroit, started in gospel and still returns to it, to reconnect with God, she said. Fontella Bass got her message from God to reenter the recording scene after a twenty-five-year absence (1960s R & B hit "Rescue Me"), and combines saxophone, barrelhouse (boogie-woogie) blues with church choir and organ for a new gospel sound in *No Ways Tired*.

A nonbeliever can get into the spirit of things via movies (and now videos), especially with the documentary "Say Amen, Somebody!," Whoopi Goldberg's "Sister Act I and II," and Steve Martin's "Leap of Faith."

If you like gospel music, a classical cousin is Handel's "Hallelujah Chorus" from the "Messiah." You might also appreciate the amazing vocal range of Mariah Carey as she sings "Emotions." If the Clark Sisters exhilarating gospel song "Hallelujah" moves you, try techno rock group 2 Unlimited's "Let the Beat Control Your Body," Mark O'Connor's "Orange Blossom Special," big band's "In the Mood," or zydeco group BeauSoleil's "Jeunes Filles de Quatorze Ans." These works generate the same positive energy through the elements of rhythm, melody, and harmony.

Soul

Soul music mediates blues and R & B, telling life stories with a moody rhythm band.

Ray Charles almost single-handedly created soul music out of black gospel in the 1950s, making it more lyrical, telling a story. After that, many singers crossed over to gospel, pop, or soul, with the lure of money, popularity, and record company deals. Aretha Franklin is now known as "Lady Soul," despite her gospel origins. "Soul to me is a feeling, a lot of depth and being able to bring to the surface that which is happening inside, to make the picture clear. The song doesn't matter. . .It's just the emotion, the way it affects other people."[4]

Soul builds a thicker texture than gospel by adding brass, piano, guitar, bass, and drums, and preaches the message of turning pain into power in songs like James Brown's "Say It Loud, I'm Black and I'm Proud," the Impressions' "Movin' on Up," Anita Baker's *Rhythm of Love* and Mary Blige's melancholy "My Life." Diana King's *Tougher Than Love* combines reggae with R & B and gospel to create energetic soul.

Ben E. King, better known as B. B. King, the "King of Soul," said his roots were in a Memphis neighborhood where "the world ceased to exist below the 110th Street subway stop." His music "started as a neighborhood thing. And your buddies. . .were your *heart*. You could get so in tune it seemed you all had but one heart between you. Those street years were the best of my life."[5] His biggest solo hit "Stand By Me" is a soul ballad that ties him to those neighborhood roots.

The emotion-laden lyrics are a major component of soul. One young woman, who at age twenty-one has seen her share of problems, told me, "My father died recently, unexpectedly, from a massive heart attack. He was only forty-six. So I've been listening to a lot of songs that say, 'I miss you, I love you.'" She had one experience which was unusual even with true-to-life soul songs. The young woman told me, 'Seven Whole Days' was the only tape I played every day when my daughter's father just up and left us. Amazingly, he came home after a week. He returned to us on the seventh day just like the lyrics say!"

In "Seven Whole Days," Toni Braxton sings of pain endured while living an entire week without word from her man. When she reaches her breaking point, refusing to endure this torment, he suddenly returns—seven days later.

If you appreciate the dark, lamenting feelings soul can communicate, try listening to the mournful "Lento" movement from Gorecki's "Symphony No. 3," with the thick texture of a full orchestra, Rapper Scarface's "I Seen a Man Die," with grimly sad lyrics or the moaning guitar and violin in Josh White Jr. and Robin Batteau's "House of the Rising Sun." "Primo Tempore" from *Officium* by Jan Garbarek and The Hilliard Ensemble evokes grief with a classical/jazz variation on a Gregorian chant, using saxophone and four tenor/baritone voices.

Folk

Folk music tells life stories and questions life values in ballad format, with thin textures and bending notes.

Folk music preceded country, much of it brought over by early immigrants from the British Isles. Called the "white people's blues," songs like James Taylor's "Oh Baby, Don't You Lose Your Lip on Me" or "Steamroller" have bending notes in the singing that tug at the listener's heart strings. One male executive prefers to listen to the folk hymn "Amazing Grace," played on bagpipes. He admitted his own amazement. "Usually bagpipes really annoy me, but when they play 'Amazing Grace' I can feel the music go clear inside me. The sense of endurance and faith come through." The bagpipes playing "Amazing Grace" at the funeral procession in front of the 1995 Oklahoma City bomb site was a moving example. The timbre of bagpipes and thin texture of one instrument reached inside us to resonate with our sadness.

Folk music has simple music elements: melody, straightforward rhythm and harmony, and storytelling lyrics, as found in "Danny Boy." During the 1930s, music historians traipsed the mountains and valleys of Virginia, West Virginia, Kentucky, and Tennessee, discovering songs from three centuries ago, not written down, just remembered and still sung. For instance, the melody for "Oh Shenandoah, I love your daughter. . ." has many, many narrative variations.

Both "Danny Boy" and "Shenandoah" are included in Soothing music selections because the elements of a sustained memorable melody and slow tempo are effective calmants. But as we'll see time and again, the human element can add totally unexpected dimensions to any music. During an impromptu violin performance at home for visitors, something (intuition?) prompted me to play "Danny Boy." One woman began crying uncontrollably. Through her tears, she talked about the suicide of her husband Danny. Her healing process was assisted as she was able to express her deep emotion. The music qualities and the lyrics seem lovely but rather sentimental to many; she brought to it her own tragic emotional identification. For her, "Danny Boy" produced memories that provided a cathartic release of Unsettling emotions.

From the 1930s onward, folk music changed with the influence of hillbilly, rock, calypso and African styles. The 1960s were exemplified by new folk singers who rediscovered the emotional elements and added political connotations. A college professor remembered the emotions of brotherhood and loyalty he found in the songs and in the singing:

> I miss the sharing of music. I miss being able to walk in a room, not just a party, anytime, where someone would have a guitar, and everybody knew the words to the song. It wasn't about dancing or listening, although those can be group experiences too, but it was about sitting close to one another, feeling close to one another, a roomful of people sharing a single mood.

Does '60s folk music inherently have that power? Not for everyone. To some, it will always remain "hippie" music; to others, it's just outdated. A twenty-seven-year-old said, "My parents were '60s people. My mom would cry at "Blowing in the Wind," really embarrassing. Well, to me as a kid, "If I had a Hammer" and all that were just great campfire songs. That pissed them off, but at least it meant we could all sing along in the car."

I classify singers Sheryl Crow and Melissa Etheridge in progressive folk because their earthy appeal, guitar-based melodies, and storytelling lyrics cross over to rock by adding electric instruments and a full-textured band sound. Sheryl Crow's "All I Wanna Do" has a melancholy feel, in "white people's blues" fashion, with a fast rock rhythm (1-**2**-3-**4**) where you really have to listen hard to the words to catch the message, similar to listening to rap. Melissa Etheridge's voice is rougher, reminiscent of Janis Joplin's, as she sings philosophical lyrics. She uses a technique of starting out with a thin texture, only guitar and voice, which generally hooks you into the music more easily. By the end of the song, as in "Silent Legacy," the band is playing full force with the fast rock rhythm.

If you like the peaceful nostalgia that much of folk music repertoire brings to mind, you may find that same emotional experience with Natalie Cole's "Unforgettable," Barbra Streisand's "Evergreen" and "He Touched Me," or Vaughan Williams' "Fantasia on Greensleeves." If the songs of Pete Seeger and Bob Dylan are meaningful to you and can evoke Unsettled emotions you need to deal with, you might also like the agitated feelings of jazz-based "Wings of Karma" from *Apocalypse* by the Mahavishnu Orchestra and Berlioz's "Dream of a Sabbath Night" from "Symphonie Fantastique." The slower music of Sheryl Crow and Melissa Etheridge is similar to the melancholy moods found on country singer k.d. lang's *Ingenue*.

Country

Country music tells stories of good times, bad times with old sounds of crying, or new sounds of rock rhythms.

Country's golden age is considered to be the immediate postwar era because of the recording industry's discovery then that a lot of Americans would buy the "old-timey sounding" records. A similar renaissance happened in the early 1990s, when it was "discovered" how many Garth Brooks' tapes and CDs stores were actually selling. This is new country.

There is a division of preference between today's country—the new country—and the older format, country-western. Those who prefer the older form respond to the steady rhythms, crying lyrics, simple melodies and harmonies, as found in Patsy Cline's "I Fall to Pieces" or Hank Williams' "Your Cheatin' Heart" and Johnny Cash's "A Boy Named Sue." Johnny Cash understands the downside of life and, in a recent article, one attorney explained that Cash's music "has better prepared me for my work as a prosecutor. It is easy. . .to despise not only a criminal act but the man or woman behind the act. On more than one occasion, prosecutors have likened various criminals to animals. Cash taught me that even a prisoner remains a human being."[6]

Today's country is different, crossing over into pop, rock, and gospel. These new music styles are attracting listeners who never used to listen to country. In both forms, the music usually matches the lyrics, for both good times, bad times, and "somebody done somebody wrong" songs. That word/music match strengthens the message for healing purposes.

Bending notes (pitches that slide up or down to communicate love or sadness) abound in country music, especially in ballads, or a "three-minute soap opera,"[7] as Johnny Hartford called it, and create heart-tugging Unsettling or Soothing music. Unsettling examples are Kathy Mattea's "Where've You Been" (sadness), Lorrie Morgan's "I Guess You Had to Be There" (ruefulness), and Suzy Boggus' "Letting Go" (loss). For Soothing emotions, try Trisha Yearwood's sentimental "Thinkin About You," Kenny Rogers' "You Are So Beautiful" from *Timepiece* and John Michael Montgomery's "Long As I Live."

One woman surprised hospital staff by refusing to have an MRI test done unless she could listen to country. Even though she's a classically trained violinist, she much prefers country for relaxation and peaceful feelings. She demanded the new country radio station. Since an MRI requires absolute stillness she had to stifle her laughter when the first song was Garth Brooks' "I've Got Friends in Low Places." That's another side of country: the sense of humor and ingenious wordplay. "If I ever get depressed about my marriage failures," said one divorcee cheerfully, "I put on 'All My Exes Live in Texas.'"

Country is also the energetic music of square dancing, swing, bluegrass, two-stepping (try George Strait's "The Fireman" and John Michael Montgomery's "Sold"). Hoedown music, with any combination of fiddle, banjo, bass, mandolin, dulcimer, mouth organ, electric guitar, peddle steel guitar, and drums, all vigorously playing away, is full of cheerful exuberance. To me, the "Orange Blossom Special" by the legendary Mark O'Connor may be the most Energizing of all. A Cajun cousin to the energetic "Orange Blossom Special" is zydeco music—always fast, with the same kind of instruments, adding the accordion.

Garth Brooks' "The Thunder Rolls" from *No Fences* and *Greatest Hits*, is definitely categorized as Unsettling (how *completely* Unsettling is described in chapter 8). If the gloomy mood of "The Thunder Rolls" works for you, try alternative rock group Counting Crows' "Perfect Blue Buildings," soul singer Sade's "Pearls" or Gorecki's "Symphony No. 3." The elements within Soothing country have similarities to Raphael's "Healing Dance" (new age), and Mickey Hart's "Mysterious Island" (new age/world). For unquenchable energy, listen to zydeco group BeauSoleil's "Jeunes Filles de Quatorze Ans," and techno rock, such as 2 Unlimited's "Let the Beat Control Your Body."

Christian

Christian music usually contains God-centered lyrics, touching people through a variety of music styles.

Christian music (also called Contemporary Christian Music or CCM), is sometimes referred to as "white gospel," to distinguish it from the traditional black gospel. The verbal distinction is one thing, the sound quality is totally different. The music has been around since the 1950s but has really gained momentum in the last five years, owing more to soft rock and easy listening styles than to the sing and sway of black church choirs.

Parents who were horrified at the sound and lyrics of heavy metal favored by their children were delighted with the burgeoning appeal of Christian music. Even if parents didn't approve, many teens and young adults would still listen. The rhythm is energetic without being driving, and joy is in the sound as well as the lyrics.

The following is a true story. It's long because it's important, demonstrating how music's power can help overcome depression at high tide, even feelings of suicide.

During 1991, Patty M., at forty-one, hit bottom. For the three years since her husband's death from bone cancer the fear of getting cancer herself had haunted her. Widowed, and a single parent of six children, ages five to eleven, Patty was too nervous to eat and compulsively overworking in an attempt to quell her fears. She was down to a gaunt ninety-six pounds, from a fit and trim 110 on her 5'1" frame. Her condition was diagnosed as severe clinical depression. Prozac and other medications were prescribed, but Patty reacted by feeling even more "high strung." Despairing, she refused the medications, sank deeper into depression, and lived with suicide as a constant temptation.

But one thing helped: the music that she loved. Patty told me she found that if she played music first thing in the morning, she would be lifted out of her suicidal thoughts. Spiritual music especially brought her closer to God and made her want to live. She listened to the Mormon Tabernacle Choir, Michael McLean, Wanda Lindstrom, and the duo Janice Kapp Perry and Joy Sanders Lundberg.

She was keeping suicide at bay, but severe neurologic pain in her neck and side and searing headaches appeared. As Patty says, she hurt, a lot, all day, every day. Then, during Christmas, her mother had a stroke and died. Patty was reeling from all of this.

"Sometimes, I thought I was going crazy. I called those relentless headaches 'brain pains.' They were so much worse than migraines and lasted day in and day out. Suicide started looking good to me again."

"I realized it was up to me to get myself out of depression. Music had helped when medication did not. 'Alright,' I said, 'more music.'" She kept music playing continuously, all day and night. And it worked. After a period of weeks, the force of the music (positive lyrics matched with joyful melodies and harmonies) changed her mood into happiness and alleviated the pain.

She was still seeking additional ways to utilize music to relieve

*stress when she came to my music therapy workshop. The work-
shop confirmed that, intuitively, she had chosen the right music to
save herself. Now she could build on that, as she learned how a
variety of her favorite music, listened to in sequence, could help her
maintain a healthy lifestyle and a rich, positive view of life itself. "I
truly believe that God utilized everyone and everything, including
music, to save my life."*

Churches have used every music style available to communicate
God's message. There is growing controversy over what "Godly"
music should be.[8] Some say "Godly music" should be musically
restrictive, deliberately avoiding the use of certain music elements,
such as repeating notes, too-loud drums, melodies creating tension
or sadness, or anapestic beats (di-di-DAH). Amy Grant is credited
with beginning the Christian music renaissance, however, in her
1994 release, *House of Love*, she definitely moved into the realm
of rock and lost a good chunk of her original audience. The most
enduring objection to Christian music seems to be that many of the
songs never go beyond saying "Jesus loves me" in a million variants, without deeper exploration into the responsibilities of mind
and heart. More positively, varying rhythms and instruments create jazz, rock, and easy listening, as in Steven Chapman's *Times
and Seasons* and Phil Driscoll's trumpet in *Instrument of Praise*,
accompanied by orchestra, drums, and chorus.

Although a specific combination of music elements might help
you attain nirvana, bliss, the kingdom of heaven, or whatever
term you identify with, it is up to each of us to intuit what music
strengthens the spiritual connection to our "Creator." Too much
satiation of "Godly music" might be repressing other emotions
which you need to express.

Kay R., a thirty-year-old Midwestern wife and mother, says,
"Listening to Amy Grant's tapes is better than watching television
because it's more relaxing. It gives me quiet time for myself." For
additional Soothing music, listen to the quiet message of country
singer Kathy Mattea's "Mary, Did You Know?" and
"Emmanuel" from *Good News*, which also features bluesy gospel
and folk music. I would also recommend the symphonic sounds
from *Instruments of Praise* by the Tom Keene Orchestra. Music
for you to USE in other styles for reaching that peaceful center

include *Chant* (classical-Gregorian), "Cool Mountain Stream" (new age-environmental), Puccini's aria "O mio babbino caro" and the instrumental "Meditation" from "Thais" by Massenet (both opera), and Mike Rowland's *Fairy Ring* (new age).

Listening to this chapter's heartfelt music styles—blues, gospel, soul, folk, country, and Christian—may put you in touch with emotions that run deep within you, emotions that may not have surfaced, or feelings that lie dormant or repressed. The next section will take us on a journey of raw energy. You will find a variety of music to USE in jazz and the 3 R's.

5

Primal Forces:

Jazz/
Rhythm & Blues/
Rock/
Rap

WHEN WRITING THIS chapter, a bit of folk wisdom came to mind; "Don't force the river, it will flow by itself." A residual core of the music we'll consider here suggests power looking for an outlet, answers demanded but not always available. If jazz, rhythm & blues, rock, and rap are not part of your musical life, then you will find vibrant energy, fascinating discordances, and unexpected sounds. If you already like one of these styles, you'll gain a better understanding of their connecting points to others. Among the emotions for you to work with are anger, depression, tenderness, and exhilaration.

Let's begin with jazz, one of the forebears of the 3 R's—R & B, rock, and rap. See if, in your opinion, one twenty-five-year-old's statement rings true: "Older generations were raised on harmony and today's youth are more interested in the beat."

Jazz

Jazz is rhythmic music, often improvisatory, which grew out of ragtime and earlier black American styles.

Jazz stimulates a variety of emotions because it has evolved through five generations of change: traditional, big band (swing), modern, free, and rock. As the predecessor of jazz, African American music included the field songs of the slaves, the street cries of New Orleans, and "cakewalks, buckwings, and jigs" from minstrel shows which then became popular in drinking houses as "ragtime" around 1890.[1] As jazz evolved its own distinctive American sound, many classical composers also became fascinated with the sound and incorporated jazz and ragtime into classical formats. Listen to Debussy's "Golliwog's Cakewalk" from *Children's Corner*, Eric Satie's "Parade," and Claude Bolling's "Suite(s) for Violin (or Flute) and Jazz Piano." As an epochal reverse, George Gershwin ("Rhapsody in Blue") and Duke Ellington later gave jazz a symphonic sound.

Traditional Jazz

Traditional jazz is Dixieland, born in New Orleans around the turn of the twentieth century.

Dixieland began as the music of the black community, played by bands for parades and funerals, as a sonorous advertisement for products by street vendors, and at social gatherings for pure entertainment. The instruments were often leftovers from the Civil War—cornets, clarinets, and trombones, which produced the recognizable bright, strident timbres of traditional jazz. Lively rhythms were created by the banjo or guitar, tuba or string bass, and drums, as the improvised melody line was played by the low-pitched trombone, high-pitched clarinet and the trumpet's fast vibrato. "When the Saints Go Marching In" is probably the best known and one of the most vigorous examples of Dixieland. This is high-energy, life-affirming music.

Big Band (Swing)

Big band or swing is primarily dance music with full brass, often with one or more vocalists. Personality cults often developed around band leaders in this style of music.

Moving on to Chicago, then New York and Harlem, jazz permeated the nightclubs (with segregated black/white clientele) that had sprung up. Brothers (and leaders) Jimmy and Tommy Dorsey, on saxophone and trombone, introduced the swing beat (1-2-3-4) of big band. By the 1930s, jazz was overshadowed as big band grew to dominance from the late 1920s to the 1940s. Personality cults and single-minded fandom developed around band leaders and vocalists like Peggy Lee and Frank Sinatra. This was music to dance to and it dominated the lifestyle of young people. As Duke Ellington summed it up in the song title, "It don't mean a thing if it ain't got that swing."

Various studies credit big band or swing jazz with alleviating the residual stress of the Great Depression and forging excitement and group unity during World War II. Goodman did danceable swing, Count Basie's music was "balls ahead" swing, and Duke Ellington painted sound with impressionistic colors. Among all of the great sounds and songs, though, it's Glenn Miller's "In the Mood" that best exemplifies those cheerful feelings with the right Energizing combination of music elements. ("In the Mood" is discussed in chapter 10.)

Today, big band music, like the folk of the '60s, evokes strong associative emotions, and we "can't get there from here" unless we listen to the music.

Psychiatrist Will L. lives in a major city where his patients come and go all day, but those conversations are specialized and devoted to the patient's needs. There are stretches of time spent alone and Will is often very aware of having no one to talk to, especially while writing, between patient sessions, and late at night.

Some of the medical theories he is interested in are controversial, which complicates the isolation. "I'm at odds conceptually with a lot of members of my profession, so there's no local support system," he says. "Music has become my support system. For me, music serves a function I can't imagine anything else doing.

"I think of myself as in the last phase of my life, and I like to go back to those years which have a more peaceful resonance for me. Listening to Benny Goodman and Artie Shaw will do that. But the comfort is only one level of value, because the more I listened, the more I became aware of Benny Goodman's artistry. I realized I was listening to a superbly gifted artist, a man with a great gift. And I find that very encouraging to my own creativity. In a tough week I'll work through all forty of my Benny Goodman CDs!"

Music that stimulates uplifting memories can release a positive flow of energy when the good feelings from good times are needed today. With big band music, even if there are no memory associations for you, you can still hear the vitality inherent in the big band sound itself. Listen to Benny Goodman's "Tiger Rag," Artie Shaw's "Frenesi," or Glenn Miller's "Tuxedo Junction."

Although the big band era ended soon after World War II, this music continues to appeal to a wide spectrum of people of all ages. Big band music belongs in Energizing ("In the Mood"—fast) or Soothing ("Stardust"—slow), depending on the tempo of the song. Rhythm is a steady 1-2-3-4. The harmonies are pleasurable, with dissonances usually created to provide contrast and interest, not tension. The timbres are predominantly brass, woodwinds, keyboards, bass and percussion, as heard in "In the Mood." The familiar big band sound texture is thick, with up to five saxophones, four trumpets, four trombones, piano, bass, and drums. This style utilizes "call-response" patterns, where the solo instrument or voice "calls" and other instruments answer or "respond." Easy-to-remember melodies hook you into participating—dancing, singing, or swaying your shoulders. You could USE big band music both for Soothing and Energizing emotions, to get, literally, in the mood.

Modern Jazz

Modern jazz music was written after 1945, and focused less on blues and more on experimentation and dissonance.

As big bands waned, modern jazz dominated the scene, from the late 1940s to the 1960s. People stopped dancing and started listening. The music was simplified to accommodate smaller bands, usually five or six instruments. Stan Kenton started writing music that jumped around, layering lines and building tension with dissonance, making the music more Unsettling, without the Energetic enjoyment for dancing.

The legendary trumpeter Miles Davis led modern jazz through the several substyles of bop, cool jazz, hard bop, and the complicated bebop (e.g., Charlie Parker's saxophone in "Back Home in Indiana"). Cool jazz is softer music, with medium tempos and irregular phrasing that lacks the blues sound. Most cool jazz borders between Unsettling and Soothing. Its West Coast variant is considered very easygoing (more Soothing than Unsettling), as in Gerry Mulligan's sinuous version of "Moonlight in Vermont" and Dave Brubeck's "Take Five" and "Rondo in Blue." Hard bop grew out of bebop, simpler yet hard-driving, with wilder improvisations, creating very Unsettled moods. You'll hear that in John Coltrane's tenor and soprano saxophones in "Giant Steps" and "My Favorite Things."

Free Jazz

Free jazz combines jazz improvisation with rock and electronics.

In the late '60s, free jazz developed and all rules disappeared. Any number of musicians were allowed to play anything without beat or melody. All but the most diehard jazz artists—and fans—grew tired of this quickly. Free jazz is Unsettling to a point where I don't even recommend it as useful Unsettling (which may be why it only lasted a few years).

Jazz Rock

Jazz rock fuses rock and funk ('70s-style rhythm & blues), adding exciting, repetitive rhythms.

Jazz rock succeeded modern jazz and moved at an ever-faster pace from Energizing into Unsettling. Both Quincy Jones' "Superstition" and Ike & Tina Turner's "Higher" make you want to move. The evolution into more Unsettling modes came with extreme electronic improvisations called jazz rock fusion. Landmark recordings were Miles Davis' "Bitches Brew," Cream's "Wheels of Fire," and Jimi Hendrix's "Electric Ladyland."

Having reached the current jazz era in time frame, I'm not sure where jazz is going, but the creativity is still there, as found in Wynton Marsalis' "In This House, on This Morning" and Christian McBride's "Gettin' to It." Even though many jazz aficionados have firmly held belief systems, jazz is "a wonderfully open and elastic music that has, in its relatively short history, absorbed energy from myriad sources."[2] Today, Eric Clapton brings blues and rock to jazz, Ry Cooder brings in island percussion/world sounds, and Pat Metheny takes cool jazz into both rock and airy new age realms.

If Dixieland music is what you like, consider Mark O'Connor's country fiddling in "New Country" from *Heroes*, Yanni's new age/jazz energy in "Swept Away," or Mariah Carey's pop vocal gymnastics in "Emotions." These selections may stimulate the same Energizing feelings.

If you like the big band sound in general, you might also like Barry Manilow's "Singin with the Big Bands" (1994) and the styling of pianist/singer Harry Connick Jr. If "In the Mood" strikes your fancy, you'll find the music elements of regular rhythms, pleasing harmony, and strong melody in Michael Franks' "Practice Makes Perfect" (jazz), Ary Barroso's "Brazil" (world), Enya's "Orinoco Flow" (new age), Bob Marley's "Soul Shakedown Party" (reggae rock), or Elton John's "The Circle of Life" (film-soundtrack).

Modern jazz lies in the grayer areas of the Unsettling, Soothing, or Energizing categories. I've noticed that many taxi drivers in large cities listen to the mellow forms of jazz, for example, Pat Metheny's *Secret Story*, as it helps them deal with traffic. If you prefer modern jazz at a fast tempo, you may also like the quick rhythms, unrelenting dissonances, and the back-and-forth tossing of musical sections to various instrument groups during "Infernal Dance" from Stravinsky's "Firebird Suite," "Festival of Crows" by new age duo Timmerman and Wise, or Janacek's classical masterpiece "Sinfonietta."

John McLaughlin's "Wings of Karma" with the Mahavishnu Orchestra is found in Unsettling (chapter 8) and is a typical fusion of jazz rock music, with the added twist of the band being backed by a symphony orchestra. The music elements of intense, irregular rhythm, dissonant harmony, erratic improvisations, and abrupt changes, create a very Unsettling mood in "Wings of Karma." Similar characteristics create a comparable mood in Berlioz's "Finale" from "Symphonie Fantastique," Gwen Mars' "Heal Me" from *Magnosheen* (rock), or "Allegro" from Shostakovich's "Symphony No. 10."

Rhythm & Blues

Rhythm & blues (R & B) combines the blues with off-the-beat rhythms and features a honking saxophone. (Note: R & B is the root of rock 'n' roll.)

Rhythm & blues was born in the 1930s–1940s, when jazz bands began playing the blues but added syncopation (accents between beats), call-response patterns, and a vocalist with a "rough, throaty voice"[1] who shouted as often as he sang. R & B music communicates intense feelings, ranging from sorrow to the joy that comes with bending notes. R & B was a confluence of blues plus gospel, making songs a mixture of Unsettling and Energizing music elements, as heard in Smokey Robinson and the Miracles' "The Tears of a Clown." Remixing the mix, British groups The Who and the Rolling Stones, who already had a driving rhythm component, added the blues to their style. The Stones' "Get Off My Cloud" exhibits the old blues shouting technique.

Rhythm & blues elements were brought into folk rock, progressive rock, and rock operas. You'll hear the R & B sound in music as diverse as Woody Guthrie's folk song, "This Land Is Your Land" and The Who's "Tommy." One fortyish executive gets a kick out of analyzing R & B influences in other styles, such as British group UB40 who "take old R & B and make it 'white' reggae." Maria G., age seventeen and Mexican, has no problem being a fan of both the late Tejano star Selena and the R & B group Boyz II Men.

R & B's emotional melange can lend confusion if it is USEd for specific emotional healing. Mixing Energizing rhythms with Unsettling, melancholy blues, R & B is telling your body that you should be ecstatic and feeling good about the downside of life. I'm not saying that R & B has no place in your healing program: memory associations linked with that music can provide an avenue for healing when other music is ineffective.

To find sorrowful feelings, listen to the slow tempo songs of minor keys and sad lyrics, such as The Persuaders' "Thin Line Between Love and Hate." You'll find similarly Unsettled feelings in Josh White Jr. and Robin Batteau's blues instrumental "House of the Rising Sun," "Perfect Blue Buildings" by Counting Crows (alternative rock), and Gorecki's "Lento" from "Symphony No. 3."

If the R & B song happens to be both slow tempo but in a "happy key," such as Ray Charles' "I Can't Stop Loving You," or in a major key with lyrics that produce contentment, as in Ray Charles' "Georgia on My Mind," then you might USE it in your Soothing collection.

Energizing emotions are easily found in the faster tempos of R & B. If you like Boyz II Men's "Motownphilly" from *Cooleyhighhar-*

mony or "Treat Her Like A Lady" by Cornelius Brothers and Sister Rose, extend your options by listening to Herbie Hancock's "Dis Is Da Drum," Michael Franks' "Practice Makes Perfect" (both jazz), "Soul Shakedown Party" from Bob Marley's reggae rock hit *At His Best*, or "Swept Away" by Yanni (new age/jazz).

Rock

Rock music, a cultural phenomenon, took over the popular music of the 1950s.

"Rock 'n' Roll" was the first incarnation. Several other forms have evolved since, so much so that rock 'n' roll, which was anathematized by the righteous in its day, only evokes nostalgia now.

Rock began in the 1950s as the casual mixing of rhythm & blues with country, which grew into a new fusion sound, rock 'n' roll. Simple lyrics and melodies, and the energetic rhythm (1-**2**-3-**4**) made immediate hits out of Elvis Presley's "Hound Dog" ("just a white boy singin' black"—anonymous), Bill Haley and the Comets' "Rock Around the Clock," and Chuck Berry's "Roll Over Beethoven." Instrumentation mixed and matched the timbres heard in country and rhythm & blues with any combination of mouth organs, saxophone, piano, guitar, bass, and drums to create an Energizing mood.

The addition of electronic instruments marked the breakout into rock music. The sound of the 1960s came with the Beatles' "Can't Buy Me Love" and the Beach Boys' "California Girls." Rock drummer Rod Morgenstein remembered the instant inspiration of "seeing the Beatles play on Ed Sullivan. From that moment, I couldn't think of anything else I wanted to do. I feel very fortunate to have a career in music. I know so many talented musicians that for whatever reason, can't seem to catch a break. My advice to anyone is: do it purely for the love of music. If nothing in terms of commercial success ever comes of it, you're still doing something you love."

Rock, which had started as a fusion itself, took on new forms. From the West Indies, **reggae** was imported. The rhythm, harmony, and melody of reggae establish a mix of Soothing and Energizing feelings. When the electric instrumentation of rock is added, results can be emotions ranging from Unsettling (melancholy) and Energizing (joy) to confusion when elements mix up USE categories. Bob Marley is perhaps the best known of the reggae rock artists and his recording *At His Best* exemplifies this range of both Unsettling and Energizing emotions *and* the confusion. Country hillbilly music merged with rock for Energizing **rockabilly**, as heard in the Everly Brothers' "Wake Up, Little Susie." The Grateful Dead moved from **acid rock** through blues, folk, jazz, and country genres. Other acid rockers led lives and played music that spun out on psychedelic trips. Jimi Hendrix, Jim Morrison of the Doors, and Janis Joplin continue to be revered, though all three acid rockers were dead by 1971. The rock beat (1-2-3-4), examples of which can be found throughout the USE categories, continues to be experimented with over the decades. Many emotions are possible, predominantly found in the Unsettling and Energizing categories.

Rock groups like Cream started jamming with extended improvisation, epitomized by the inventiveness of Eric Clapton. Thus, **heavy metal** was born, a rock substyle whose Unsettling music elements include intense volume, emphasis on the electric guitar, and maximum improvisation. Metallica, Iron Maiden, Kiss, Alice Cooper, and Black Sabbath's Ozzy Osborne maintained strong followings into the 1980s. Heavy metal's satanic messages, whether deliberate or not, fueled the Moral Majority's uprise against this music and it lost momentum in the 1980s.

Punk rock entered the scene just after heavy metal, continuing the fascination with pompously satanic themes and adding agitating, screeching elements. It was an attention-getter in the mid-to-late '70s and was popularized during the early '80s. Punk rock groups and singers, for example, Cyndi Lauper, David Bowie, the Sex Pistols, the Clash, and Adam Ant, made a point of shocking mainstream society whenever possible, exhibiting a lot of frustration, anger, and stage presence along the way (definitely Unsettling moods).

Slam dancing became the rage and got unruly enough to occasionally disconcert performers. Having been shaken by a bad experience at one concert, the group Dead Milkmen were prepared at the next. After watching a belligerent slam dancer being escorted from the nightclub in a headlock, they said, "We hate to leave on such a violent note," and finished the concert with a more relaxing Jamaican ska beat.[3] Punk rock violence literally became overkill; when everyone was doing it, it was no longer news. Green Day, Offspring, and Bad Religion kept the sound but toned down the violence. Black Flag's lead singer Henry Rollins crossed over to alternative, still anger-driven, but lower key.

Glam (glamour) rock became a substyle of heavy metal in the mid-1980s with a lot more sex, a lot less violence, and male stars wearing extreme makeup and skin-tight pants. Motley Crue and Poison could be considered personifications of the style. Even though glam rock sounded like heavy metal on Valium, it never crossed from Unsettling emotions to anything Soothing. Glam rock was short-lived, a product of the music recording industry's hunger to find a new niche to popularize. I'd put Madonna in the glam rock category, but she crosses over into many rock styles and employs a variety of USE emotions, creating what she likes. Her songs tend to be controversial, which in itself lends an emotional mix. The healing value may be found in a variety of USE emotions, depending on your identification with her. She's her own niche.

Today, **classic rock** is something of a stylistic catchall. It includes hard and soft rock and the niching together of older artists, among them Sting, the Doors, the Rolling Stones, Bruce Springsteen, the Eagles, Led Zeppelin, the Grateful Dead, The Who, Pink Floyd, Aerosmith, Steely Dan, and Tina Turner. The Doors are an example of how classic rock stays alive, arranging Jim Morrison's old poems to new music on *An American Prayer*.

Rock can be judiciously USEd for healing, but be discriminating in what you choose. If it's "your music" and you identify with it, both relaxation and positive energy are possible. The rhythm and improvisations work for you as accessible Unsettling music. Classic rock gives you the most USE options.

Massage therapist Karol C. has been practicing and teaching for over fourteen years. "I use music to prepare myself before working on a client. One of my favorite tapes is Tina Turner's 'Simply the Best,' because it has a deep rhythm I can feel. It gives me the energy and timing I need to work on my clients, who are primarily athletes with complicated musculo-skeletal problems."

Tina Turner's **pop rock** sound can evoke a variety of USE emotions. The element of Turner's R & B styling is most likely what

Karol was referring to as she flexed and strengthened her own muscles to give deep massage. New age music comes later, to relax the client.

More rock substyles have surfaced in the '90s: **industrial, techno, house, trance, alternative, grunge,** and **roots.** Frank V., age twenty-five, works in a major record store, owns over 500 CDs, and has a ceaseless appetite to hear rock sounds that identify different feelings. "When I was a teenager I listened exclusively to heavy metal. My mom didn't like the friends I hung out with or the music we all liked, so she created pretty hard times. When I was in the Navy for four years (including the Gulf War) I learned not to prejudge music until I really listened to it. Moving back and forth between the East and West coasts I sampled friends' music of alternative, industrial, and techno rock."

As soon as it wasn't his Mom dictating "he must," Frank started branching out into other music on his own. My only concern is that the music styles he mentioned limit him to Unsettling and Energizing emotions. He lacks the Soothing category.

Industrial was imported from Europe in the mid-to-late '70s when German rock artists such as Kraftwerk and Gary Numan brought computer-generated rock music to the United States. (The computer age in music had actually begun in 1928, when classical musicians in Germany first became fascinated with the sound potential of electronics.) The American version of industrial music comes from the early '80s, in the Southwest, adding sounds of construction scenes layered with electronics. Definitely Unsettling music.

In the early '90s, industrial group Nine Inch Nails progressed (actually, it seems to be a returning) from strictly electronic to live guitars and drums. "The music became more real with people transferring feelings of frustration through their instruments so the audience could see and feel the frustration better."[4] Nine Inch Nails' release *Downward Spiral* achieved hit status and considerable respect among Generation X fans, who cited its honesty about the effects of depression. One song, "Hurt," is a passionate rock lament over the suicide of the band's drummer. Although the lyrics start out aggressively, by the end, says one Generation Xer, he experiences with these lyrics a cathartic release of his own personal depression: "If I could start again a million miles away I would find a way." If you already like industrial, this music is very good for matching the Unsettled mood of depression. Listeners who are not into this sound should look elsewhere for mood-matching music.

Free-style entered the rock music scene in the mid-to-late '80s as an inner city sound that appealed cross-culturally to white, black, and Latino listeners. Preteens and teenagers buy the upbeat, fast-paced pop freestyle popularized by Trinere and Debbi Deb. Freestyle has a repetitive, catchy tune, good rhythmic beat, and a fast, heavy bass line that characterized the mid-to-late '80s. It can be USEd as Energizing music.

In the '90s, **techno** surfaced from European dance **acid house rock** of the '80s, played for a feel-good party atmosphere. At a slamming tempo of 140 bpm, it's very-high energy and exhilarating. 2 Unlimited's "Let the Beat Control Your Body" is an example from the Energizing list. Techno combines electronics with hip-hop (rap + jazz, described later under rap). You didn't dance to techno, you "raved" at underground parties with easy access to amphetamines and designer drugs like Ecstasy. "Rave" parties were held anywhere from abandoned tunnels in Germany to the West Side piers of New York City, and the hottest clubs. Like techno's tempo, techno songs move fast, from instant success to a quick fade within weeks.

Computer **techno** bore a substyle in the urban Chicago/Detroit areas when it fused with the jazz/rap sound of hip-hop (and elements of classic R & B). Labeled "house" (a cousin to acid house rock), it's an energetic dance or '70s style disco music, as one producer described it, " 'Saturday Night Fever dance rock." To catch the sound and see if the energy level works for you, listen to New Order's *Substance* or Marshall Jefferson's *Sweet Sensations*.

Now **trance** (aka **ambient techno**) has surfaced and a new "natural high" is sought with amino-acid energy drinks. A fan described these new sounds of sustained notes with very little tempo and rhythm as "more ethereal, closer to new age. Listening to Orb or Aphex Twin is like a mind journey. I've read that Aphex Twin actually creates his music while in a sort of zombie state." Trance belongs in the Soothing category for many people because of the long sustained mid-range notes and lack of rhythm, as found in Autechre's "Windwind" from *Incunabula*.

New wave started around the same time industrial hit the United States. It was called "synth pop" or "Euro pop" and also used electronic music, or computerized sounds, to evoke emotions of either Unsettling or Energizing (anxiety-driven or happy), rarely Soothing moods. One recent example is Depeche Mode, a new wave group who brought darker emotions and sexual overtones into ballads to create distinctly Unsettling music. I did find a Soothing possibility: The Cure is known for its colorful softer sound, as heard in "Lovesong," similar in sound to the new age group Tangerine Dream.

Alternative rock is the mainstream to Generation X (the current term for age twenty somethings), who are not at all fazed by alternative's Unsettling moods and can listen for hours to the music of Counting Crows, Elastica, or Bjork. Too many in this age group have experienced the breakdown of the family as a cohesive unit, with all its related problems. Grunge, the leading alternative rock style, embraced that angst theme (lyrics match music) and a generational fashion statement: the Northwest working-class look of flannel shirts and scruffiness, which became a fashionable look.

Another Generation Xer is convinced that alternative rocker Lenny Kravitz projects love to everyone in his music. "I can always bring friends out of bad trips from acid rock or mushrooms with Lenny Kravitz."[5] Although Kravitz's mixed fashion statement is '70s disco style—big flared pants, glitter vests, and dreadlocks, his songs carry words of breaking down barriers between whites and blacks with the message "believe in yourself." There are religious overtones in his ballads and even in the heavy, guitar-driven rock.

Grunge is the Seattle sound of Nirvana, Soundgarden, and Pearl Jam, with Stone Temple Pilots catching the style in San Diego. Scotty, mid-twenties, grew up without a father and listens to Pearl Jam's Eddie Vedder when he's in a down mood because he feels a strong identification with Vedder. "He came from a broken home and didn't know who his dad was. He prefers not to explain the song's lyrics so that his fans can pick out the meaning that means something to them. Then they don't feel left out if they don't identify with a true meaning. 'Jeremy' is about a kid at school who's constantly ridiculed and can't explain his frustration to his parents because they just don't understand. The song ends in violence. Someone gets killed, but it's up to you as to who it is."

Many fans felt the group Nirvana had answers for the problems of the human condition. Then, in 1994, Kurt Cobain, lead singer/guitar player, committed suicide. Joey Ramone of the Ramones has said he misses Nirvana's "soothing, calming effect, their soul and spirit and angst, great songs, antics, and excitement. Where are the exorcists [music of suicidal depression or hard-driving fast tempos with guitar and vocal distortion] when you need them to calm the beast within?"[6] If you connect with Nirvana's music, I trust you'll find part of the answer to that as you expand your music collection to USE music more effectively.

Another substyle of alternative is **roots rock**, akin to the sounds of Bruce Springsteen and John Mellencamp. Roots rock groups include regional bands like Hootie and the Blowfish, the Dave Matthews Band, Big Head Todd and the Monsters. The record industry has noted that many bands are "taking on a multicultural character. Mr. Rucker (Hootie's lead singer) is black; the Dave Matthews Band is fronted by a white South African and includes many black members. Hootie and the Blowfish have been called the 'heirs of the '60s,' mixing new age spirituality with traditional values in their album *Cracked Rear View Mirror*."[7] A Generation Xer is sure that alternative rock still has a lot to offer "as long as new lyrics and music continue to be produced."

The variety of intense emotions produced by all of these rock styles can match moods predominately found in the Unsettling category. If you like heavy metal, punk rock, industrial, and grunge, try listening to the dissonance in Timmerman & Wise's "Festival of Crows" (new age), "Wings of Karma" by Mahavishnu Orchestra (jazz/rock), "Heal Me" by Gwen Mars (rock), or Shara Nelson's "Pain Revisited" (popular).

The driving beat of rock styles such as rockabilly, reggae, classic rock, techno, and house may generally be found in the Energizing category. For similar upbeat emotions, try the nonstop fast pace of the Cajun group Buckwheat Zydeco's "Zydeco Boogaloo," Mark O'Connor's country-style "Orange Blossom Special," the happy rhythm and singsong melody of jazz artist Michael Franks' "Practice Makes Perfect," and the joyful drumming in Nicholas Gunn's new age "Odessa."

Trance/ambient techno and roots rock may be considered Soothing by many listeners because of the slow, sustained notes and lack of rhythm. Also, although heavy metal is classified as Unsettling, there is ongoing research to support the fact that this music can create Soothing effects for those who have a strong gut-level response to it. For other types of music that generate mind-mellowing feelings, try *Chant* by the Benedictine Monks of Santo

Domingo de Silos (classical-Gregorian), Jean Michel Jarre's *Equinox*, or Raphael's "Healing Dance" (both new age). These convey calm, contemplative moments of peace and relaxation.

Rap

Rap is a repetitive style of music that describes the day's events, in the words of one scholar, built on "long-standing black cultural forces" that "dissolve the past and the future into one eternal present, in which the passing of time is no longer noticed."[8]

In 1986, the Beastie Boys—punk rockers before becoming rappers—had the first rap music release to top the charts. "The early rap had no bad words," claims one rap lover. Since then, dozens of rappers have appeared, many named with "MC" (Master of Ceremonies), employing a disc jockey (DJ) (who provides turntable effects like rhythmic scratches, backward and forward sounds bites, and snatches of prerecorded music), a drummer and a keyboardist. M.C. Hammer's *Please Hammer Don't Hurt 'Em* stayed at number one for half of 1990 and is strongly antidrugs and antiviolence.

Fans and detractors cross racial boundaries. Maria, a teenager, says, "Whether I'm in a good or bad mood, rap works." Rap psyches her up to fight back and solve a problem, or [this with a laugh] "It makes me want to party." Ice Cube is her favorite rapper. To the sympathetic ear, rap is an expression of a way of life with Unsettled feelings of frustration and anger coming through loud and clear. I asked a father what he thought about his son's love for rap, and he surprised me: " Rap is okay—especially the way rockers Walter Becker and Donald Fagen use the same beat with more profound lyrics." Further conversations revealed that both father and son harbor the same angry feelings about the condition the world is in.

A young music producer said, "Mine was the only white family in a black neighborhood so I can really identify with a lot of the rap message [frustration]. I still listen to the Beastie Boys when I want to pick myself up when I'm down [depressed, unhappy, or blah]."

The Beastie Boys and others have progressed to hip-hop—which is jazz plus rap, rap's anapestic beat with a jazz feel—and carried their fans with them. Rap took on these jazz intonations in the late '80s, as heard in Us3's "Cantaloop" from *Hand on the*

Torch. One traditional rap lover enthused about hip-hop, "The lyrics cover more issues, not just about one guy's day, but about society's problems in general."[9]

Listeners new to this style could try Us3's "Cantaloop" (jazz quintet accompanying rapper Rahsaan), the Beastie Boys, and Digable Planets (a New York trio with horns and DJs). On the outer edge of the rap spectrum is hard-line gangsta rap, epitomized by Dr. Dre, Ice Cube, and the late Eazy E. Digital Underground went in the other direction—goofy, but with a strange sense of fun, rather than rapping about serious issues.

Some supporters liken rap to the protest songs of the '60s, insisting that, eventually, a social commentary on the '90s may acknowledge the social truths behind many rappers' words. Quintessential rap features a black male rapper (more black females are now getting into it as well) who comments about life and work conditions, expressing strong sentiment in the timbre (tone quality) of the voice. Rap fans get a rush singing the lyrics quickly, along with the rapper. The texture of rap is thin, with usually just the rapper's voice, drums (usually electronic), edits from other records, and sirens, house noises, and conversations in the background. The voice and instruments are without any audible vibrato (no heart-tugging stimulus), so the rapper's own intensity and lyrics are left to move you. Meanwhile, the repetitive anapestic beat will either hook you or come across as really aggravating.

The violence that is typical of today's rap, the foul language, and the often belittling attitude toward women in the lyrics polarize listeners: you love it or you hate it. Gangsta rap is seen as a clear and present danger. Recent commentary by Senator Robert Dole concluded that, "A line has been crossed, not just of taste, but of human dignity and decency. It is crossed every time sexual violence is given a catchy tune, when teen suicide is set to an appealing beat."[10] Snoop Doggy Dog, Dr. Dre, Cannibal Corpse, and Geto Boys were cited as major offenders, with several record companies seen holding onto gangsta rap only for profit. One company refused to distribute a gangsta rap recording, yet continued to promote heavy metal music, which, to many, can be as offensive as gangsta rap. William Bennett, the former secretary of education and bestselling author of "The Book of Virtues" and The Moral Compass" also asked the music industry to act responsibly. "We're not talking about censorship. We're talking about citizenship."[11]

Rap music holds a valid place in today's music, and I would definitely put it in the Unsettling category. I do not, however, recommend gangsta rap USE within the mood-matching system. As discussed on the national front, society's problems can be perpetuated within the expression of gangsta rap. The extreme negativism has to stop, and yes, it can be done. Read the lyrics of rapper Scarface's "I Seen a Man Die," in chapter 8. There's real dignity there. He talks about real life, hard life—without the demeaning, hate-filled lyrics. If you do like rap you'll find similarities in "Pruit Igoe" from the soundtrack for the film, "Koyaanisqatsi," and Mahavishnu Orchestra's "Wings of Karma" from *Apocalypse*. Both match angry moods less intensely while allowing listeners to vent feelings of frustration.

> **Caution:** As a music therapist, I get concerned when I see only one kind of any music in a collection, more so if it's all in the Unsettling category.

The controversy over rap leads to a related consideration. Both rock's denigrators and people who genuinely care about the state of the music they love share concerns about the effects of lyrical content and certain types of rhythms. These effects increase if the music is listened to for a long duration. Acid rocker Jimi Hendrix said, "You can hypnotize people with music, and when you get people at their weakest point, you can preach to them into their subconscious what we want to say."[12] This worries some rock artists; others view it as part of the game. It is your personal responsibility to judge what is most healthful for you.

This chapter has an evolutionary, this-happened-after-that pattern, and I do not want to end abruptly with rap and some of the more disturbing nuances in rock. Like the group Dead Milkmen, I too "hate to leave on such a violent note." It is important at this point to remember that music has always been a forum for social expression and a medium of exploring many of society's emotional states, whether they are good or bad. It would be equally wrong to focus on the darker recesses of current music as it would be to demand music that's always happy and fun. That said, I can lead you into the next chapter by promising that the going will be easier, both in content and in musical effect.

6

Pride and Prejudice:

Popular/
Easy Listening/
Film & Stage/
Classical/
New Age/World

CERTAIN MUSIC STYLES tend to receive simplistic attention, from the intellectual conceit that popular music requires no brain strain, or new age is for airheads, to the "I hate classical music" that pops out defensively from someone threatened with a piano sonata. (Yes, I could have put rock and jazz here, as well. Any number of classical music lovers have said peremptorily that they loathe rock. Jazz is dismissed by many as "noise," as is rock.) No form of music is too "easy" or too "difficult" to find enjoyable, if we don't push our own automatic reject buttons. Within this eclectic grouping, you will find emotions of anxiety, grief, tenderness, relaxation, joy, and enthusiasm.

Popular

Popular music is a marketing concept as much as it is a style. It's music that is easy to remember, with a strong melody, contagious rhythm, and equally easy-to-remember lyrics.

"Popular" music evolved in the Middle Ages, in the days of troubadours roaming the countryside and village streets, offering to sing the favorite songs of the people. In the 1800s, popular singers were seen in "pleasure gardens" and "supper rooms."[1] The public came to enjoy sing-alongs in music halls and vaudeville, or stayed home with friends and family around the piano.

Popular music retains its popularity because the music stays in your head. The memorability factor gives popular songs distinct individual associative values, songs that make you "remember when": "Cheek to Cheek," "Over the Rainbow," "Love Me Tender," "It's Wonderful, Wonderful," "Here Comes the Sun," "Mandy," "Lady in Red," and "Raindrops Keep Falling on My Head" are just a few of the thousands of popular songs.

During the 1970s, popular music also assimilated another element—the energizing disco rhythm. Any and all styles, from classical to country to jazz could be connected by dance DJs, who added the disco rhythm, which emphasized all four accents equally. This rhythm, coupled with the predominant tempo of 120 bpm, conforms to the body's natural rhythm. This conformity made the disco rhythm easy to move to at the 120 bpm pace, or twice as slow so that one could still be "in time" to the music. The 120 bpm tempo exactly doubled that of the 60 bpm heart at rest. The music's beat felt natural. As examples, listen to Donna Summer's "Love to Love You Baby," "MacArthur Park," or "Last Dance."[2] You could USE this music to pick you up when you're feeling blah.

The disco rhythm waned in the late '70s. The main feature of today's popular music is the continuing crossover into stylistic variety, incorporating soul, blues, folk, rock, jazz, and country. Popular music in all eras tends to be purposefully light, and to be successful songwriters must still create those memorable melodies and lyrics. One L.A. songwriter, however, Diane Warren, has written over forty Top Ten hits for, among others, Celine Dion, Michael Bolton, Gloria Estefan, and Elton John, but says her basic nature is anything but light.

"I'm not really an emotional person. I have a pretty sick sense of humor. . .In real life I'm very cynical and sarcastic." She is considered one of the most successful writers of pop songs because she gets past that intellectual framework and is able to find "something I love, something emotional with great melodies and lyrics that can really touch people. . .that will last through the ages. The best ones are the ones that make me cry when I'm writing them."[3] I found strong echoes of borderline sadness (Unsettling) and love (Soothing) in her music.

Popular music is generally categorized as Soothing or Energizing, unless a particular song reminds you of a specific bad time. For you, that song will be Unsettling. There are other exceptions as well. Listen to "The Rose" and you may find a grieving mood already, and European pop star Shara Nelson's "Pain Revisited" directly matches an agonizing Unsettled mood. For Soothing music, if you're in a loving mood, try Gloria Estefan's "Live for Loving You" or Michael Bolton's "How Can We Be Lovers," the new age tenderness of Narada artists' "The Cello's Song" from *A Childhood Remembered*, country's "You Can Sleep While I Drive" by Trisha Yearwood from *Thinkin' About You*, or Kenny G's "Sentimental" from *Breathless* (jazz).

Operas are full of love—desired, won, or lost. Intermezzos, the emotion-laden music played between acts, will almost always be Soothing or mildly Unsettling in an "oh, what might have been" vein. Dubious nonopera types will find many collections of arias and intermezzos from which to sample. The aria, "O mio babbino caro," from Puccini's "Gianni Schicchi" is one of the main Soothing choices.

If Elton John's "I'm Still Standing" energizes you, try also Mariah Carey's "Emotions" (popular), "Presto" from Beethoven's "Symphony No. 7" (classical), "Just One World" from Craig Chaquico's *Acoustic Planet* (new age, sounding like new country), or Michael Franks' "Practice Makes Perfect" (jazz).

Easy Listening

Easy listening music is a conglomeration of music styles, intentionally Soothing.

The term *easy listening* suggests just what it is: music that is easy to listen to, without being Unsettling or too Energizing. Your body doesn't receive a strong message to jump around or shake an angry fist. This section of easy listening focuses on lush orchestral arrangements of mellow melodies without words, although music arrangements may be thick with texture (orchestras) with an unobtrusive drum beat. Listen to Cole Porter's "Begin the Beguine," especially Artie Shaw's big band version, or "I've Got You Under My Skin" by Michel Le Grand & Orchestra.

Easy listening is also a record store's catchall for artists whose songs are not classified as pop/rock/soul, are not on the Top 40 charts, or who have a mix of softer-sounding music styles. Popular songs, as well as artists who have a mix of styles, find their way into easy listening when they become "dated." Originally produced as record albums or tapes, many easy listening artists are reformatted for CD and repackaged to look current.

"Muzak" began decades ago with easy listening music to calm anxious claustrophobic elevator riders, thus the derisive name "elevator music." Today, with 150,000 cataloged songs, that bland background music has come "out of the elevators and into the '90s"[4] to appeal to the baby boomer. According to Jeff Ferguson, Muzak programmer, "contemporary jazz instrumentation of guitar, keyboards, bass, saxophone, drums, and flute replaces yesterday's sounds of 101 Strings." Heidi W., age twenty-nine, works at a major hotel's restaurant which pipes in one of Muzak's foreground music channels. "Michael Bolton, Madonna, and Salt-n-Pepa keep me and our diners happy. It makes me love to work." Ferguson said Muzak's research has also identified physiological/psychological slumps during the work day so they have background music segments designed to boost workers with tempos that match desired energy levels.

"Norwegian Wood" (a collection of Beatles' songs) by Trio Roccocco (oboe, cello, harp) and "Wind Beneath My Wings" (popularized by Judy Collins and Bette Midler) by Richard Clayderman, are examples of easy listening music without lyrics that cross over into classical and pop styles that may affect you as Soothing and mildly Energizing. If you like easy listening you might also enjoy the calming effects of "Fantasia on Greensleeves" by Ralph Vaughan Williams (classical), Mickey Hart's "Mysterious Island" from *Planet Drum* (new age/world), "Forever" from the *Edge of Forever* by Hilary Stagg (new age), and "Instruments of Praise" by the Tom Keene Orchestra (Christian).

Film & Stage

Film and stage music effectively match a wide range of USE moods through a variety of music styles.

This section of record stores is really expanding. The composers have honed their ability to stimulate public emotion through music to match the visual effects. It is becoming a cliché that Broadway success currently depends on Andrew Lloyd Webber and revivals of hit musicals from the past. Considering this, one composer enumerated: "Gershwin, Lerner and Loewe, Kurt Weill, Rodgers and Hammerstein, Bernstein. These are the greats, these composers have defined the best. Anyone else who follows will be doing some kind of copy of them. These composers are like Bach, who summed up everything in music that had gone before him."

I would hope there are still more great musicals to come. We need the emotional inspiration of heart-tugging music and drama or comedy that captures an audience's imagination. Anyone who has been touched by the great stage songs recognizes the unabashed emotions in them. If a song touches you, USE it to bring about that mood within yourself.

Film music covers an immense range, and I'll name just a few songs that have outstanding emotional constructs that would make it easier for you to bring about a desired emotion. One of the best mood-matching, and scene-setting uses of classical music was Rachmaninoff's "Piano Concerto No. 2" as the sole background for the 1940s four-handkerchief film classic "Brief Encounter." The music matches the movie's emotions of passion, loss of love, and restlessness. Even hardened film students sniffle, and may learn to like classical music.

The 1993 film "Fearless" spiked Gorecki's "Symphony No. 3" into instant stardom. The music's brilliant evocation of the Unsettling emotion of mourning makes it a primary choice in that category. Prokofiev's scoring of Eisenstein's films in pre-World War II Russia, especially "Alexander Nevsky," created film and music history. Nevsky's "The Battle on the Ice" is very Unsettling; the entire film is stirring, energizing. Bernard Herrmann wrote intense, sinister music at Hitchcock's and Truffaut's behest, and you'll definitely find Unsettling music in a collection of his film scores. Luckily, there are such collections; in those days there were few soundtrack releases made for films that weren't full-blown musicals.

Today, when an original score is not commissioned, the music analyst on the film will pick from the best of many genres of music: pop, rock, world (ethnic), R & B, jazz, classical—whatever it takes to match the on-screen emotions. The best scores will cue the emotions even without the visuals, but if you saw the movie and can remember the scene your emotions will be even stronger.

"The Lion King" soundtrack is a Disney success, topping 1995 charts with music that evokes emotions from sadness to happiness, especially for those with children. Whitney Houston's soundtrack for the film "The Bodyguard" (with Kevin Costner) has already sold over 32 million copies worldwide because the music stirs up memories of the movie, and the individual pieces have strong USE components, from love of God to dancing joy. "Room with a View," "Sleepless in Seattle," and "Philadelphia" stand out as recent soundtracks which also give you different mood-matching music with which to work.

Among the interviews for this book, one in particular is memorable because of its focus on a pet who benefited from an owner's positive emotions. Norma G., a children's book writer, discovered years ago that her mood also becomes her dog's mood. Tasha is her Norwegian Elkhound. "When my husband and I are laughing, Tasha will smile, showing her teeth and wagging her tail till it falls off. When we're full of joy, she's full of joy." (Tasha can't see their joy, only hear it. She is blind, from glaucoma.) "We lived in an apartment when Tasha first became blind, and I became the 'guide' dog in maneuvering the stairs. That was when I became so conscious that dogs really rely on their owners and a certain trust develops. I become her mate, her cohabitant. I am her life partner."

The dog lies at Norma's feet as she works. "Listening to music helps my writing and when my writing is going well, Tasha can sense it." Norma fine-tunes her writing to music, looking for "music that really hits my heart" to improve the sensitivity of her work. Pavarotti's vocal collections, Puccini's operas, and the song stylings of Sammy Davis Jr., Celine Dion, and Roger Whittaker, as well as soundtracks, are part of her music collection. " 'The Sound of Music's' 'Climb Ev'ry Mountain' and 'The Music of the Night' from 'Phantom of the Opera' are two of my favorites."

Is the music healing, helping Norma's dog? A kennel in England purposefully USEs the music of Bach to quiet barking dogs.[5] We don't know, however, if Norma's music directly effects Tasha. We do know the music helps Norma, who then communicates her happiness to the animal companion who loves her. That communication has a way of healing both.

Classical

Classical music spans 400 years of formal design, composed for solo, vocal, and orchestral compositions that stimulate a wide range of USE emotions.

Composer Milton Schafer said, "To me, classical music is simply the imposition of formal design on wonderful melodies—it's definitely intended for people to listen to and be emotionally touched."

A broad range of feelings can be produced by this music. The various time periods of classical music create substyles, each of which has its own emotional content and sound: the Baroque era (1650–1750), the Classical era (1750–1830), the Romantic era (1820–early 1900s) and twentieth century music. The period prior to the Baroque was the Renaissance, newly popularized through Gregorian chants.

Schafer loves the Romantic era of classical music because it expresses his true nature. "I played it at concerts and it is a part of my own temperament. Rachmaninoff (a Romantic composer) was not an innovator, but he created glorious sound, tides of emotion. If I'm feeling fine, and nothing's bugging me, I love the cascades of sound found in Romantic music. However, when I'm not feeling well, this kind of music is too much a deluge of sound, too turbulent. If I'm in trouble physically—aches and pains—I'd choose Bach piano, and Mozart piano and string quartets."

Classical music is performed many different ways, using large to small groups or a single instrument. Symphonies maintain very thick textures with forty to eighty musicians. Examples: Brahms' "Symphony No. 4 in E minor" and Tchaikovsky's "Symphony No.

5 in E minor." Chamber groups are smaller, averaging two to twenty musicians playing pieces with thinner textures. Vocal music can be heard on a grand scale as part of larger orchestral pieces, choral works, and opera. Examples: "Ode to Joy" in Beethoven's "Symphony No. 9 in D minor," Handel's "Messiah," Mozart's "Requiem," and all of opera, with Bizet's "Carmen" being an easy beginning point for opera, because so much of this music has been popularized. The symphonies mentioned here vary in USE because the emotions change from Unsettling to Soothing to Energizing, as the movements change.

"The Mozart Effect"

Specific music from the Classical era (1750–1830—not all classical music) has been found to effect the brain's performance. After a single session of listening for ten minutes to Mozart's "Sonata for Two Pianos in D Major, K.448" college students were much better able to perform spatial reasoning tasks. For comparison, the researchers also tried minimalist (electronic) music, a spoken story, and trance (ambient techno rock) music. The results of this study imply that the symmetry, the balance of music elements, of Mozart's composition helps improve spatial response ability. The improvement times, however, were short-lived, curving off fifteen minutes later. That accompanying result took the fire out of the media hoopla over "the Mozart effect," but has encouraged further research.[6]

Specific music from the Baroque period has been found to produce the alpha state of awareness, which is used to facilitate learning. For the most effective results, three components are recommended.

- Tempos around 60 bpm (our resting heart rate) as in "largo" sections from the music of Vivaldi, Bach, Handel, Telemann, and Corelli.
- The music of stringed instruments.
- Instrumental music without lyrics.[7]

Don M., a hospital administrator, learned from attending different health care meetings that, "Music therapy works. Not sure of which direction to go for my long-term patients, I decided to start with myself, and bought a tape of Baroque medleys. I was excited to discover that my usual short attention span was lengthened with this music. It helped me to concentrate better when reading or studying as well as ignore outside distractions."

None of the classical composers need to be justified by their "USEfulness." However, you can listen to Beethoven for emotional intensity of anger, calm, or joy, Haydn for cheerful elegance, Schubert for both lighthearted poetic lyricism and heart-tugging sorrow, or Mozart, usually for Energy, secondly for Soothing, rarely Unsettling.

The Romantic period is usually exemplified by the descriptive music extolling love and nature, exemplified by Liszt, Chopin, Mendelssohn, Berlioz, Tchaikovsky, and Rachmaninoff. Brahms, Bruckner, and Mahler symphonies have Romantic essences, although their intense dramaticism is the most evident quality, evoking strong Unsettling, Soothing, and Energizing feelings. The grand operas of Wagner's "Ring Cycle" and Verdi's "La Traviata" were written during this time period and embody great heights of every emotional USE. Composers drew on the "music for the people," too, bringing folk melodies into classical structure, for example, the nationalist music of Tchaikovsky's serene to bombastic "1812 Overture," Sibelius' sweeping "Finlandia," Dvorak's "New World Symphony" and Smetana's "The Moldau." The moods of music are deep and intense in this era and can serve an effective variety of USE because of the concentration of music elements, such as very loud to very soft notes, memorable melodies, whether hazy or distinct, and soothing-to-quick tempos.

Conceptualized by Schoenberg and enthusiastically followed by Ives, Stravinsky, and Varese, twentieth century classical music appeared as 'new music,' without regard to previous traditions: the atonal (or nontonal) style with pitches that have no minor or major key. Composer Easley Blackwood gave up "writing in atonal idioms." He described the effect of atonal music as "brass screaming away in a high register, the strings scraping up, in a cacophonous, ugly sound. Even if it's played accurately and correctly, the effect can be unnerving. There's now a whole repertory of that stuff. You don't hear it very often, for obvious reasons."[8]

Amongst the cacophony, I have a fondness for Charles Ives

(1874–1954). He developed all of his new music attempting to depict the earthly chaos around him. He once wrote to his copyist, "Mr. Price. Please don't try to make things nice. All the wrong notes are *right*."[9] Ives' own life was fraught with pain, and as hard as he tried to compose, it often proved impossible. This type of atonal music can be USEd to match Unsettled feelings of irritation.

On the lighter side of Unsettled, twentieth century music, Swedish composer Jan Sandstrom was commissioned to write "Cantos de la Mancha (Songs of La Mancha) for Trombone and Orchestra." Based upon "Don Quixote," the music score itself looks like a cartoon—on paper and during the performance. "This mind-map is the only way I could communicate how to play the visions seen by Don Quixote," says Sandstrom. Solo trombonist Christian Lindberg says the therapeutic value in performing "Cantos," "is in the physically demanding tragic humor. I feel a great release after yelling, singing, and jumping around as I follow the mind-map with the orchestra." Since I was involved in a performance of "Cantos" myself, I have renewed hope for twentieth century music.

The jarring effects of atonality that typify twentieth century music would have both amazed and pained the creators of Gregorian chant, one of the earliest forms of music. The Gregorian chant of the Benedictine Monks of Santo Domingo de Silos in the CD *Chant* is a recent outstanding example. In a chant, the flowing interchange of minor and major keys usually evokes tranquil feelings. Chants such as this may be listened to for pure Soothing enjoyment. Chanting as a music form may include atonality and has been used for centuries in many cultures for pain deferral and spiritual benefit. African tribal rites use chanting to concentrate inner strength for moving enormous weights. Far Eastern chants prepare devotees to walk barefoot through a track of burning coals. Native Americans chant to induce "trancelike states before entering into various painful initiation rituals."[10] Zen Buddhist monks in Japan chant atonally to confuse and disarm the rational mind, to prepare the mind for experiencing deeper levels of meditation.

Rather than disarm the mind, the Gregorian chants of the early Catholic Church are meant to center, to ground the listener. The combination of music elements in the CD *Chant* can be mesmerizing. It has the right pitches, melody, texture, harmonies, durations, timbres, and vibrato. This best-selling CD seems to appeal to every age group, from teenagers to seniors, and has brought about new interest in the music of Josquin des Prez and Hildegard von Bingen (the latter a twelfth-century nun, feminist, mystic, and composer of echoing musical poetry).

I use a wide range of classical-style music in my own therapy work, and will share one participant's comments:

It was like I have been blocked all of my life. I didn't hear. Music was just noise. I only listened to music when I was growing up, popular music. Now [after initial music therapy] I feel like I am being healed. I feel freer inside, I can soar with the music. Not only that, but things inside of me are starting to move and change. I feel peaceful.

—Patti J.

My interviews found another animal companion owner who says her cats respond directly to music, as well as to her own emotional shifts, like the dog Tasha. Jeannie T. noticed that music with brass instruments hurts her cats' ears, but that everything else— even drums and percussion—is just fine with them. "Style is most important—classical and easy listening standards. Instrumental gets better results with them than vocals. I consciously use music when my animals have to be kept inside during the winter because they don't have the usual opportunity to race around. Soothing music like Tchaikovsky's 'Sleeping Beauty,' Rimsky-Korsakov's 'Scheherezade' calm both the cats and myself simultaneously."

Arthur H. is an example of on-the-spot effectiveness with classical music. He had to visit the dentist for an emergency root canal procedure. "After forty-five minutes, the dentist realized the tooth was much worse than expected and the anticipated time in the chair was going to double, to one and one-half hours! So I demanded a radio be placed right next to me on the dental chair and turned up the volume on the local classical radio station to focus my attention. I'm convinced it took away the sensation of pain as well as diverted my attention from the problem."

Classical music has such depth and breadth of emotion that it can meet your criteria for Unsettling, Soothing, and Energizing moods. You'll find many examples in Appendix A and B at the end of this book. Professional orchestras and recording companies have made it easier for you to USE the music by creating CDs to match these different emotional states. Among the many recordings that build music around emotions are: the Cincinnati Pops Orchestra's *Fiesta* (joyfully Energizing), *(James) Bond and Beyond* (excitingly Energizing), *Chiller* (fearfully Unsettling), and *Amen* (calming to exhilarating gospel). The Boston Pops has *Pops in Love* and *Marches*. CBS created *Masterworks Dinner Classics* and Sony's *Musical Meals*, both series matching different moods to specific dining ambiences, from gourmet meals to picnics.

Opera is most often placed with classical music in record stores, but for opera lovers it has a life of its own. Nonopera lovers approach it warily, knowing only that "it ain't over til the fat lady sings," a phrase I cannot track but which has become idiomatic for not counting your chickens before they hatch. The dramatic story lines of operas take the listener through all kinds of emotions, even within one song. You'll find "soap operas," in "La Traviata" and "Il Trovatore" (Verdi), "Carmen" (Bizet), "Manon Lescaut" and "La Boheme" (Puccini), "Werther" (Massenet), and "Cavalleria Rusticana" (Mascagni), to name just a few. The four operas in Wagner's "Ring Cycle" tell a complex, mythic tale of implacable gods and high-minded heroes. His "Tristan and Isolde" is based on one of the most doomed love affairs even written. Mozart wrote "Don Giovanni (Don Juan)" about the man who epitomized love-'em-and-leave-'em. Rossini wrote the bright and cheerful "Barber of Seville" and Mozart did the "second chapter" of the same story—or what happened when they didn't live happily ever after—in "The Marriage of Figaro." You'll find cheerful music and comedy in "Marriage" too, but also songs of lost love and betrayal.

A recent study revealed an intriguing anecdote. Gaetona Donizetti's (1797–1848) "Anna Bolena" and "Lucia di Lammermoor" have some of opera's greatest scenes of mental breakdown. A recent report from the Yale University School of Medicine hypothesized that the effectiveness of these portrayals was due to the composer's own psychotic illness. The report theorized that Donizetti's brain disease contributed to the music he created in 1835 for the powerful "mad" scene in "Lucia," and the "musical and dramatic terms [of] Anne Boleyn's historically corroborated mental disorder during her imprisonment within the Tower of London."[11]

This book is not intended to exhort you to listen to any one style of music, rather that you learn to appreciate the possibilities of healing inherent in all kinds of music. If you're dubious about opera, but open to new ideas, there are short-form opera "highlights" recordings and a number of all-instrumental opera recordings—no singing, just the most popular melodies from the composers' total output.

You would recognize many that have been popularized. "O mio babbino caro" is an example, used in commercials and an audience favorite in the film "A Room with a View." Totally Soothing and graceful, it represents the composer's sense of humor, since the beautiful melody is in fact the song of a daughter begging her father to help her boyfriend commit a crime, or else her boyfriend will leave her. Energizing short opera pieces include "La donna e mobile" from "Rigoletto," the "Toreador's Song" from "Carmen," the triumphant march from "Aida" (all those elephants), the joyful wedding march from "Lohengrin"—the list is long. The soaring melodies, which in the opera correlate with a high point in the plot line, will match a range of emotions you'll want to USE for your healing program.

> If you have a PC, you may soon be able to become an "instant genius." Sony is developing a new music game where you create your own compositions with "an inventory of folk melodies, Bach inventions, and Beethoven chord progressions."[12]

New Age

New age music is often a mix of instruments, synthesizers, and/or nature sounds, without lyrics or memorable melodies, intended to quiet the mind, as well as crossovers from jazz and world styles of music that create Energizing fast rhythms.

New age music began in the mid-'60s as minimalist music, in reaction to the unpopular "modern classical" music, or atonal music. Minimalism created rhythmic patterns underneath simplistic, trancelike short phrases of notes that repeat with gradual changes. At the same time, the 1960s counterculture of hippies and flower power was exploring altered psychedelic states, stimulating interest in mysticism and the haunting melodies of the East, and creating a demand for what became "new age" music. Paul Horn recorded calming solo flute music within the Taj Mahal *Inside* (1968), and later, *Inside the Great Pyramid*. Steven Halpern began his journey teaching educational seminars about music and its relaxing value.

Concurrently, English rock groups King Crimson, the Moody Blues, and Pink Floyd were introducing 'cosmic rock.' Pink Floyd's "Echoes" (*Meddle*, 1971) was for many the best of their best, blending synthesized textures of "crystalline space" that soared "to another plane of (peaceful) existence."[13] King Crimson's lead guitarist Robert Fripp teamed up with Brian Eno to produce the beautifully tranquil *Evening Star*. Eno, a minimalist, continued to produce mood-evoking environmental music "intended to induce calm and a space to think."[14] Philip Glass, an early minimalist, has recently merged minimalism with Indian ragas performed by Ravi Shankar in *Passages* and, with this, we go full circle. Shankar had recorded with classical violin virtuoso Yehudi Menuhin back in the 1960s.

European developments of new age music, which usually evokes relaxed feelings, in the '70s and '80s included the German trio Tangerine Dream, who initially played American rock music. Influenced by Pink Floyd and classical composers Liszt, Debussy, Wagner, and Sibelius they began creating a cosmic synthesized music that evolved into *Phaedra* and *Rubycon*. France's Jean Michel Jarre achieved international reputation with *Equinox* and *Oxygene*. You will find Greek-born Vangelis' "Chariots of Fire" (from the film of the same name) both in the film-soundtrack and new age sections in record stores. Japan's new age master Masanori Takashi, better known as Kitaro, has described his present-day music style as an evolution, based on personal religious experiences.

Distribution companies for music with healing potential started popping up in the early 1980s. Recommended companies include Narada, Windham Hill, Platinum Disc Corp. (environmental *Relaxation* series), Higher Octave Music, and Real Music.

Electronic music is taking on a new frontier. The brain is challenged by computer-generated music with sounds it has never heard. The late Frank Zappa, a rock performer and composer, welcomed the technology to create music that was impossible to play with traditional instruments. "I have a perfect reproduction of a classical guitar on the computer, and I can write notes that aren't on a real guitar," he had said. "I can also make those notes occur at speeds that humans just can't play. I've written plenty of stupid little songs so human beings could play 'em. Now it's time to take advantage of what technology has to offer and try to do the other stuff."[15]

Synthesized music with lack of memorable melodic lines allow you to USE new age music as a mellowing background. Pitches, harmonies, and timbres are pleasing to the ear, and many times the music is endless with no break between selections, so as to not interrupt a meditative or creative work state. If you like the Soothing feelings produced by Vangelis and Jean Michel Jarre, try listening to the tranquility of Raphael's "Healing Dance," James Galway's flute in "Song of the Seashore" (both new age/world), Pachelbel's "Canon in D" (classical), "I've Just Seen Jesus" from *Instrument of Praise* by Phil Driscoll (Christian), or trance group Autechre's "Windwind."

New age music classified as Soothing usually lacks a rhythmic pattern, although music crossovers into African music (where rhythm dominates) are intended to induce a trancelike state, such as Scott Fitzgerald's *Thunderdrums*. Depending on your response to what you hear, new age usually belongs within the Soothing and Energizing categories. However, "Festival of the Crows" by Timmerman and Wise is one new age work I've discovered to be definitely anxiety-producing, which is not a negative comment but an indication that it can be USEd for mood matching.

World

World music represents the social and spiritual life of diverse cultures.

"The pioneering sound researcher, Alfred A. Tomatis found that different cultures hear and speak in wholly different frequency ranges. How people hear determines their body posture, mental attitude, and view of the world. In many ways, what we hear is what we are. Through our technology, the music from every part of the world is now instantly available to us. We are listening to sounds that expand our ears. Hopefully it will expand our views of ourselves as well."[16]

World (ethnic) music is becoming an important key in transcending racial and cultural boundaries. The crossovers that are merging some of the music of worldwide cultures are also a factor in creating global harmony. If you discover you like Philip Glass' *Passages*, a mixture of Soothing and mildly Energizing music, you've just been introduced to Indian raga music and opened your heart to understand a portion of that culture. There are literally thousands of different ragas, each used in reference to different times of day and season. You might try listening to this music while meditating, to achieve an easier inward focus.

When South American star Luis Miguel performs in Las Vegas, Soothing and Energizing crossover styles (rock/Brazilian, etc., with Spanish lyrics), lure Latino music fans from the area and all the way from Mexico.

The Chieftains' recent release, *The Long Black Veil*, with rock lead singers, introduces Celtic lovers to a new variant we might call "Celtic rock." What a wonderful new experience to hear Tom Jones sing the tender "Tennessee Waltz" and to hear the Rolling Stones jamming with the Irish traditionalists in the enthusiastic "Rocky Road to Dublin," using additional fiddles, keyboards, and Celtic instruments. This CD has a variety of healing USEs.

Ry Cooder (who is also a part of *The Long Black Veil*) merged blues and African rhythms in *Talking Timbuktu*. "Soca" music is a joining of *soul* with *calypso*. "Salso Africana" is a new term for Spanish flamenco with West African rhythms, found in *Songhai 2*. Australian Music International's *Nomad* is an energetic merging of Africa's stamping beats with Australia's didgeridoos, vocal chants, and flute. For interested new listeners, sampler CDs are now available in world music. Lyrichord produces a "World Music Sampler" of music, including Costa Rica (calypso), Spain (gypsy), and Korea (traditional court music), which corresponds to a variety of USE emotions. Depending on your entrainment factor with these styles, the slower music may relax and calm you, the faster rhythms may make you move, and unfamiliar music may either intrigue or irritate you because the music doesn't match your cellular circuits' conditioning.

Much of world music is an inherent part of a country's religious practice: Music of the Buddhist rites in Tibet and religious ballads of Islam from Pakistan may entrain you into peace. The timeless and trancelike harmonies of African music may bring you tranquility. "Klezmer" music is the joyful Jewish folk music, which starts out slow and increases in speed. Many listeners would recognize the sound as "just like 'Fiddler on the Roof.'" As you listen to other countries' music, remember they do not have Western classical music roots. The harmonies, rhythms, and durations may feel strange to you—unless something deep within you causes that entrainment factor to kick in.

China's music was once played at solstices and important festivals with *10,000* musicians during the T'ang Dynasty (A.D. 618–907). Chinese music is categorized into yin and yang, which allows the balancing of predominant energies considered female and male. Beethoven's "Symphony No. *5*" and Bach-Gounod's "Ave Maria" would probably have been classified as yang (Energizing or masculine) and yin (Soothing or feminine), respectively. Heavy metal is (for most) definitely an Unsettling yang. Japanese music is very lyrical, with voices singing in a wide vibrato. You might especially enjoy discovering the Japanese group Kodo, for a very dramatic Energizing experience of drumming, performed with drums of all sizes. One woman, desperate to calm her baby while driving her car, found that if she played Kodo's music at the same volume that matched her baby's crying intensity, he would immediately stop crying. After the baby listened for several minutes, the mother was able to follow it with familiar music from the Soothing or Energizing categories, which kept him happier.

African music is predominantly percussive, and the rhythm inherent in this music is one of the most highly evolved. Melodic instruments and voices use the call-response pattern, as in American folk and R & B. The music varies depending on the national or tribal origin, but all Africans use it for ceremonies, social events, and communication—such as talking drum warnings. Western music's elements of harmony, and instruments such as the electric guitar, have influenced today's African music, creating high-energy urban music like West Africa's enthusiastic "high-life" and South Africa's joyous "kwela."

The world seems an appropriate stopping point in consideration of music's diversity. Although there isn't enough room here to delve deeply into theory or into all of the variants in each music style, these chapters will give you a sense of the possibilities and

Music

and

Emotions:

KEYNOTES TO YOUR INNER SELF

7

Universal Music:

What
Works for
(Almost)
Everyone

CERTAIN MUSIC WORKS for almost everyone. Appreciation of music is highly personalized, but some music simply speaks to the human condition. We cannot always say why, but we know it when we hear it. Much thought and caring has gone into this compilation of music, with qualities that will have healing value for almost everyone. The unavoidable hitch in the universality of this healing value is that certain music may cue emotion-laden remembrances. When the associations are negative, they can spoil the most wondrous sound. For most of us, though, there are fundamental music selections that will stimulate healthful physiological and psychological influences on the body. These are the basics with which you will work.

Twelve selections, four works in each of the three emotional groups, will be discussed in this chapter. The first group, Unsettling, corresponds with emotions to escape from; the second group, Soothing, contains stabilizing, soothing inner transitions; the third group, Energizing, resonates with the positive places we all want to reach.

Before you consider these works, be mindful again of what USE means and the inherent benefits of this gently therapeutic approach to music.

"Unsettling" does not equate with being "wrong." It concerns emotions that are inescapably part of facing life as a human being, emotions which need to be acknowledged and worked through before you can truly release them. "Soothing" indicates emotional states that you may want to achieve for their own value, and stay with, or emotional states you'll USE as way stations to higher energy goals. "Energizing" includes the physical and psychological vitality modes that brighten the world around us.

Each USE category can be further analyzed into specific emotions that match specific music. The emotions suggested here are guidelines for your personal exploration. You may discover that you respond to a particular music selection with a slightly different emotion. Even though you may decide, "This music feels more like fear than sadness (Unsettling), makes me more contented than sentimental (Soothing), sounds more playful than exciting (Energizing)," you will most likely agree that the music belongs in that particular USE category. Just as tempo markings for a piece of music have a range (e.g., largo—slow—is 42–66 bpm), because musicians will bring various energies and interpretations, our designations for USE need to allow some leeway. If not exact, the match should be close. USE the music accordingly to satiate, neutralize, or change your mood.

We'll begin with Unsettling for logical procession, realizing that, perhaps too often, we have refused to face these emotions, or have felt there was no relief from them. Remember, too, that you need only listen to enough to match your mood requirements.

The Unsettling Group

GRIEF

MUSIC SELECTION:	"The Rose" (3:30) (popular)
COMPOSER:	Amanda McBroom
INSTRUMENTATION:	Vocal, piano, strings

Commentary: One woman, Margaret A., chose this piece of music to listen to dozens of times, to express her grief when a loved one died. Although Bette Midler's is the most familiar version of "The Rose," the recording at Margaret's fingertips was an Awakening Heart Productions' tape, *Spirit of Love.* She would play the music over and over until she could stop crying, and planned many listening periods like that. After several months of crying to this music, she decided she was cured of her grief. Months later, during a church service, the soloist began to sing "The Rose." Margaret immediately started crying hysterically right in the middle of the church service. So much for being "cured" of grief at that time. Today, it no longer affects her to that extreme, having done its job as a cathartic tool to release the grief of her trauma.

With "The Rose," the composer impeccably matched the music to the meaning of the words. On top of the piano's entrance of slow repeated notes, the female vocalist sings the words along a slow melodic line. The listener feels the heartbreak in the music as the desolate words describe the pain of love as a razor that wounds the soul or moves like a forceful river, drowning a fragile blade of grass.

The music continues to develop more harmonies with strings and other vocals, carrying the listener through lyrics that describe what happens to a human being afraid of emotional growth, a heart that defends itself against the chance to dance with joy.

After this passage the vocals begin in a higher pitch as the music draws the listener in, the lyrics portraying a lonely night and an endless highway. Then the music quiets to feature the piano again as the vocalist sings the final message, of springtime, when the sun's love turns the seed beneath the snow into a rose. In this arrangement, the song ends as it begins, with a piano solo playing repeated notes.

There are many arrangements of "The Rose." The one that most moves you will depend on what vocalist, music style, or instruments you prefer. Beautiful vocal recordings include those by Bette Midler, Conway Twitty, and Judy Collins. Instrumental versions are performed by Gheorghe Zamfir (panflute), James Galway (flute), Jazz at the Movies Band, and Starsound.

If you like "The Rose" (in any format) you might also be

moved by "Adagio Lamentoso" from Tchaikovsky's "Symphony No. 6 Pathetique" (classical), Josh White Jr. and Robin Batteau's "House of the Rising Sun" (blues), Jan Garbarek and The Hilliard Ensemble's "Primo Tempore" from *Officium* (classical-Gregorian and jazz), Sade's "Pearls" (soul), "Lento Sostenuto" from Gorecki's "Symphony No. 3" (classical), or k.d. lang's "Outside Myself" (country/popular/folk).

DEPRESSION

MUSIC SELECTION:	"Funeral March" (9:43) from "Sonata No. 2, Opus 35" (classical)
COMPOSER:	Frederic Chopin (1810–1849)
INSTRUMENTATION:	Solo piano

Commentary: This piece exudes depression, sadness, and melancholy. The dirgelike rhythm immediately evokes images of the funeral setting, using solo piano to focus on the tragic melody. The pitches are low, lacking the optimism of higher notes.

Chopin, half Polish and half French, wrote this piece of music at the age of twenty-seven, after his first love affair had ended. He had fallen in love with the teenaged daughter of family friends and had connived a secret engagement. Then Chopin fell seriously ill and foreign newspapers erroneously announced his death. In the ensuing fuss, the secret engagement was discovered and called off. Chopin fell into a deep despondency, mirrored in this music.

This piece embodies the essence of Chopin. Although he loved company and company loved him, his letters to close friends revealed his underlying moods of intolerance and anger, which he masked with politeness and apathy. He only allowed private feelings and thoughts to be expressed through the piano, more so than any other composer working with any other single instrument.

Almost ten minutes long, the "Funeral March's" duration may seem interminable. As with medicine, take as needed; short doses are allowed. Other music that may match this mood include the Beatles "I Want You" from *Abbey Road* and Peter Gabriel's "Mercy Street" from *So* (both rock), Counting Crows' "Perfect Blue Buildings" from *August and Everything After* (alternative rock), Scarface's "I Seen a Man Die" from *The Diary* (rap), or

Garth Brooks' "The Thunder Rolls" from *No Fences* or *The Hits* (new country).

ANGER

MUSIC SELECTION: "Pruit Igoe" (7:02) from "Koyaanisqatsi" (film)

COMPOSER: Philip Glass

INSTRUMENTATION: Chorus, orchestra: woodwinds (flute, clarinets, saxophones), brass (trumpets, French horns, trombones, tubas), lower strings (viola, cello, bass), piano

Commentary: Listeners feel a mixture of anger, fear, panic, and agitation. This film is a photo/film montage of natural disasters, created without dialogue or narrative structure. The word "Koyaanisqatsi" from the Hopi language means "a world out of balance." As one cataclysm follows another on screen, a Hopi prophecy is sung throughout the film. The prophecy forecasts worldwide disaster if man continues to drain and deplete the natural resources within the earth. The music sustains and enhances that fatalistic message wherein man drives himself relentlessly to his own end, to what the Hopi call the "Day of Purification" when "cobwebs" cover the skies. Then volcanoes will erupt, throwing ash all over the planet, covering land and sea with lava and scorching countries as oceans boil. "Koyaanisqatsi" presents these natural disasters to scream for a life change.

Glass caught the prophecy's apocalyptic mood in "Pruit Igoe" with a somber opening that transitions to relentless brass and chorus. The rest of the orchestral instruments join the brass to back up the chorus with a pounding, vindictive march. The finale of "Pruit Igoe" releases the explosive energy of the chorus and orchestra through sustained lower notes, but the release is one of exhaustion, carrying the listener into a solemn balance and a more melancholy mood.

Glass, a classically trained musician, is interested in how electronic technology correlates with the function and structure of human beings. He composes music to match one's emotional potential. "Pruit Igoe" is the sound of human life gone awry.

If you respond to "Koyaanisqatsi," other possible music aids for you might be Mahavishnu Orchestra's "Wings of Karma" (jazz rock), Berlioz's "Dream of a Sabbath Night" from "Symphonie Fantastique" (classical), "Betrayal and Desolation" from the soundtrack of "Braveheart," Gwen Mars' "Heal Me" (rock), Prokofiev's "The Battle on the Ice" from the film "Alexander Nevsky" (classical), or Shara Nelson's "Pain Revisited" from *What Silence Knows* (popular).

ANXIETY

MUSIC SELECTION: "Mars, the Bringer of War" (7:26) from "The Planets" (classical)

COMPOSER: Gustav Holst (1874–1934)

INSTRUMENTATION: Full orchestra

Commentary: People tend to feel warlike while listening to this music, which is exactly what the composer intended. The piece deliberately evokes feelings of anxiety and tragedy. Holst used dark, booming bass beats to open the piece, adding a grim, low melodic line introduced by the horns.

After a brief lull, the lower strings introduce a sustained melody. Meanwhile, the higher strings and brass build crescendos that herald the return of the menacing rhythm heard in the beginning. The piece ends with intense, piercing high notes from the brass accentuated with lower pitches from all of the other instruments.

Holst began to compose "Mars" after a friend introduced him to astrology. He was so impressed with each planet's clearly defined character that he composed music to express contrasting characteristics of all the planets, including the peaceful "Venus," the hearty "Jupiter," and the mystic "Neptune." It took him two years to finish this work. It would prove a crucial two years. Ironically, Holst began "Mars, the Bringer of War" in 1914. The first public performance of "The Planets" was scheduled during World War I.

For music that evokes a similar mood of anxiety, you might consider Janacek's "Sinfonietta" (classical), "Allegro" from

Shostakovich's "Symphony No. 10 in E minor" (classical), "Festival of Crows" from Timmerman and Wise's *Poems of the Five Mountains* (new age), Wagner's "Ride of the Valkyries," or "Infernal Dance" from Stravinsky's "Firebird Suite" (both classical).

The Soothing Group

RELAXATION

MUSIC SELECTION:	"Canon in D Major" (4:55) (classical)
COMPOSER:	Johann Pachelbel (1653–1706)
INSTRUMENTATION:	String orchestra, organ

Commentary: Pachelbel's "Canon" is recommended for and has proved beneficial in many healing situations. I am not recommending the "Canon" as a panacea for all ills, but it is frequently mentioned in the therapy literature and in my interviews. It strikes a chord of healing for many people.

The bass line introduces the foundation by repeating the same eight notes in the tempo that matches the heart at rest. The violins and violas improvise melodies around eight similar notes (comparable to singing "Row Row Row Your Boat" in rounds, where each group starts in a different place).

Simple-sounding, the "Canon" is in fact very intricate. The violins and violas maintain separate, interwoven entrances. There are smooth, continuous melodies, tight harmonies, and pitches that stay in mid-to-low range. All of these combine (as described in chapter 2) to help organize the mind into a more positive mental health. Optimally, the "Canon" is played at about 60 beats per minute (one beat per second) to induce a stress-free state. This speed, the beat of the heart at rest, is the best condition for mental refocusing and learning.

Pachelbel was a pioneer in matching music to moods. He believed that a rising series of arpeggios (running notes) created exaltation; that steadfast faith sounds a repeated note, and that joyful moods resound in major keys, melancholy in minor keys. This mode of musical expression was uncommon then but is standard today.

Categorized as a Baroque composer, Pachelbel died in 1708 having had two wives, seven children, and a respectable but uninspiring career as a composer and church organist. Most of his music was liturgical and was seldom heard outside church vestries. Then, the "Canon in D" was "discovered" in the 1970s, almost 300 years later. One radio host, forced to play it too often due to listeners' requests, began to announce it as "the dreaded Pachelbel 'Canon'." It numbed him, as it does a large number of musicians now who tire of playing it. Alternatively, to many listeners, Pachelbel's "Canon" has come to symbolize a moment frozen in peace.

Today, it is available in a variety of recordings, enhanced with sounds of nature or extended play, as in Daniel Kobialka's "Timeless Motion." Music that evokes the relaxed state of conscious awareness is usually found in the classical genre, including "Adagio" from Saint-Saens' "Organ Symphony in C# minor," "Largo" from Vivaldi's "Winter" of "The Four Seasons," Debussy's "Clair de Lune," and Bach's "Air on the G String." Other choices to consider are James Galway's "Song of the Seashore" (world/new age), Autechre's "Windwind" (trance rock) and Windham Hill's *Path: An ambient journey* (new age).

SENTIMENTALITY

MUSIC SELECTION: "Ballad Theme" (2:45) from "Rhapsody
                       in Blue" (classical/jazz)
COMPOSER: George Gershwin (1898–1938)
INSTRUMENTATION: Piano, full orchestra

Commentary: After "Rhapsody in Blue" was first performed, in 1924, with Gershwin himself as soloist, it was hailed as one of the most significant works in twentieth-century music. This success followed Gershwin's first attempt to use jazz in a classical setting, in a one-act African American opera called "Blue Monday." Paul Whiteman, another orchestra leader, heard "Blue Monday" and asked Gershwin to write a longer jazz composition for orchestra for a special all-star concert. The result was "Rhapsody in Blue."[1]

In the middle of "Rhapsody in Blue," after the first long piano solo, the full orchestra enters with the Soothing, slow "Ballad Theme," first played by the strings and winds with emotional bending notes, then answered by the brass in the call-response pattern typical of blues. The solo violin enters to restate the theme, which is then taken over by full brass and a continuous snare drum roll, to heighten the drama. The piano then improvises around the theme with slow dramatic flair. The ballad ends in silence, which is then broken by the piano's sudden statement of the melody in fast, punctuated, repeated notes—changing the mood from Soothing to Stimulating.

Raised on New York's Lower East Side, Gershwin loved the blues, rags, and spirituals that poured out of the City's black nightclubs. When he was twelve, his family finally acquired a piano and his formal music lessons began. At one point, Gershwin had asked Irving Berlin for a job as an arranger and a musical secretary. Berlin told him, "You are too talented to be anybody's arranger. You are meant for big things."[2] Both as composer and pianist, Gershwin was interested in merging classical music with popular songs. A contemporary described Gershwin's playing as "a completely different music world from ours, and we did not completely understand it at the time, though we all reacted to it instinctively."[3]

Gershwin teamed up with his brother Ira and other lyricists to produce such works as the opera "Porgy and Bess," the symphonic poem "An American in Paris," and such memorable melodies as "Fascinatin' Rhythm," "I Got Rhythm," "Embraceable You" and "The Man I Love." Gershwin was an American phenomenon: his first piano at age twelve; playing piano in music stores to pitch popular songs at sixteen; and his first huge hit at just nineteen, "Swanee."

Other works that produce similar feelings are the aria "O mio babbino caro" from Puccini's "Gianni Schicchi" (opera), Trisha Yearwood's "You Can Sleep While I Drive" from *Thinkin' About You* (new country), Dvorak's "Slavonic Dance No. 2, Op. 46" (classical), Kenny G's "Sentimental" from *Breathless* (jazz), and "The Music of the Night" from Andrew Lloyd Webber's "Phantom of the Opera" (stage).

SERENITY

MUSIC SELECTION:	"Liebestraum No. 3" (4:57) (classical)
COMPOSER:	Franz Liszt (1811–1886)
INSTRUMENTATION:	Solo piano

Commentary: In a research study completed decades ago, this piece's melodic line was judged as the best to relax the most listeners into a Soothing mood. The "lingering, romantic melody is intense yet serene in expression,"[4] beginning slowly with lower pitches, and harmonies rising and falling within the melodic line. The rhythm is almost unnoticeable, as the music carries the listener through soothing arpeggios on solo piano.

"Liebestraum No. 3" is Liszt's most popular of the three compositions of this name ("Love Dream," literally), which he created in his thirties while residing in Paris, influenced by friends who were artists and writers. Liszt is considered the inventor of the symphonic poem. This passionate music was an evocation of Ferdinand Freiligrath's poem *O Love As Long As You Can Love.*

Although Liszt wrote "Liebestraum No. 3" for piano only, this work can be found today in many different arrangements, for example, in performances by the First Piano Quartet, the Boston Pops Orchestra, or strings-only recordings with nature sounds mixed in. If you like the serenity of "Liebestraum No. 3" consider listening to Mickey Hart's "Mysterious Island" from *Planet Drum* (new age/world), "Forever" from Hilary Stagg's *Edge of Forever* (new age), "I've Just Seen Jesus" from Phil Driscoll's *Instrument of Praise* (Christian), or "Cool Mountain Stream" from Platinum Disc Corp.'s *Relaxation Series* (new age-environmental).

TENDERNESS

MUSIC SELECTION:	"The Cello's Song" (7:03) from *A Childhood Remembered* (new age)
COMPOSERS:	Kostia and David Arkenstone
INSTRUMENTATION:	Violins, viola, cello, keyboards, percussion

Commentary: Rhythmic, synthesized chimes introduce and support the cello's melodic line that immediately moves into moods of loving tenderness. Running arpeggios of harplike sounds then enter, with the melody developed by soft, synthe-sized, lower pitched brass and woodwind. The cello, other strings, and winds continue to weave patterns of the melodic line. Again, you'll find here the 60 beats per minute tempo and rhythms of the heart at rest.

I recommend this Narada recording that features other artists composing and performing a variety of emotional music, sup-ported by matching visual imagery stories which are printed in the accompanying notes. Other favorite pieces are "Crow and Weasel" (sounds of Native American drumming and Indian flute strengthened with synthesized timbres and textures) and "First Flight" (a Celtic melodic line with strings, keyboards, harp, and intermittent bird sounds).

For music that evokes a similar mood as "The Cello's Song," try "The Swan" from Saint-Saens' *Carnival of the Animals* (classical), Streisand's "Evergreen" from "A Star is Born" (film), "Ave Maria" by either Bach-Gounod or Schubert, and Brahms' "Lullaby" (all classical), or Natalie Cole's "Unforgettable" (easy listening).

The Energizing Group

FROM AGITATION THROUGH
PHYSICAL EXHAUSTION TO EXHILARATION

MUSIC SELECTION:	"William Tell Overture" (7:40) (classical)
COMPOSER:	Gioacchino Rossini (1792–1868)
INSTRUMENTATION:	Full orchestra

Commentary: The first five minutes of this music may take you through the first two USE groups as the music matches first agita-tion (Unsettling), then a state of exhaustion (easily Soothed). The final (almost) three minutes change into an exhilarating, fast tempo for the entire orchestra, where the "Lone Ranger Theme" stimulates images of galloping away on a horse. The strings per-form a ricochet bowing during the memorable melodic line, alter-nating with the brass' bright passages, all of which imitate the famous gallop. Most people are stimulated into a state of energy, thereby changing fatigue into "get up and go."

Rossini was the idol of Venice, Italy. His music was so popular that the courts of law "forbade citizens from singing, humming and whistling" one of his arias ("Di tanti palpiti" from "Tancredi") in the streets because the melody had become a nuisance![5]

Rossini debuted the "William Tell" opera in 1829, when he was at the peak of his creativity and fame. The opera as a whole was not a success, then or now, because it was too long and most of the music was frankly, dull. It was his last opera; over a nineteen-year period he had composed "The Barber of Seville" and thirty-seven other operas. Rossini once said he could take even a laundry list and set it to music, and, unfortunately, many of his librettos were as functional as a laundry list.

This overture, however, is one of the most popular symphonic works performed today, and generations of radio and TV fans of the Lone Ranger can still sing, hum, and whistle that tune. If you like the energy in the "William Tell Overture," then also consider "Let the Beat Control Your Body" by 2 Unlimited (techno rock), Mark O'Connor's "Orange Blossom Special" (country), "Flashdance. . .What a Feeling" from "Flashdance" (film), The Clark Sisters' "Hallelujah" from *Black Gospel Explosion* (gospel), or Sousa's march, "Stars and Stripes Forever" (classical).

CHEERFULNESS

MUSIC SELECTION:	"Celestial Soda Pop" (4:37) from *Deep Breakfast* (new age)
COMPOSER:	Ray Lynch
INSTRUMENTATION:	Synthesizers, piano, guitar

Commentary: Rhythmic visions of "Celestial Soda Pop" popping begin the music and continue throughout the piece. Harmony and timbres blend, until the melody is introduced with the same popping sounds. Most people experience happiness—and a strong desire to dance! Lynch is a modern composer and performer who is meticulous about every sound he creates, infusing strong emotion with balanced precision. With the tools of multi-track recording and electronic sound synthesis, the album *Deep Breakfast* went gold as a best-seller.

For similar cheerful feelings, try Enya's "Orinoco Flow" from *Watermark* (new age), Scott Joplin's "The Entertainer" (jazz-rag-time), Michael Franks' "Practice Makes Perfect" from *Dragonfly Summer* (jazz), "In the Mood" by the Glenn Miller Band (jazz-big band), "Circle of Life" or "Hakuna Matata" from "The Lion King" (film), or Ary Barroso's "Brazil" (world).

JOYOUSNESS

MUSIC SELECTION:	"Espana" (6:20) (classical)
COMPOSER:	Emmanuel Chabrier (1841–1894)
INSTRUMENTATION:	Full orchestra

Commentary: Chabrier's character is reflected within his music: genial and dynamic. In a French salon full of elegant women, Chabrier played with such zeal that the instrument ended up "in a blaze of broken strings, hammers reduced to pulp and splintered keys."[6]

The brisk, even rhythm of strings playing pizzicato (plucking strings) begin "Espana." The winds join them immediately to establish the happy melody. Decrescendos and crescendos dramatize feelings of renewed joy throughout "Espana," by USEing varying timbres and volume. The trumpets give way to horns, which give way to even softer instruments until the melody is barely discernible. "Espana" weaves its way through the orchestra, tossing the melody back and forth with sweet sustained notes or punctuated brass and percussion, trading spots with winds and strings. The finale is a sweeping crescendo of brass, percussion, strings, and winds, ending in several quick chords.

Chabrier did not have a conventional music education and disdained much of nineteenth-century traditional French music. Initially a civil servant in Paris, with a few years of piano lessons, he became a composer after traveling to Germany to hear Wagner's "Tristan and Isolde" in 1879. The opera ignited his own desire to compose. A visit to Spain gave him the inspiration to write "Espana."

For similar joyous feelings, try Herbie Hancock's "Dis Is Da Drum" (jazz), Craig Chaquico's "Just One World" from *Acoustic Planet* (new age/new country) Nicholas Gunn's

"Odessa" from *The Sacred Fire* (new age), or Mariah Carey's "Emotions" (popular).

ENTHUSIASM

MUSIC SELECTION: "Presto" (3:48) from "Symphony No. 35 in D major—The Haffner" (classical)

COMPOSER: Wolfgang Amadeus Mozart (1756–1791)

INSTRUMENTATION: Full orchestra

Commentary: Most people discover new, unexpected feelings of enthusiasm when listening to "Presto." Beginning with subdued energy, the piece quickly transitions into a *moto perpetuo,* which Mozart said should be played as fast as possible.

Mozart, a child prodigy, began his career early with harpsichord lessons at age four. He had written his first symphony by age eight. As an adult, however, his golden days ended. He was paid only for what he wrote on commission for the social and religious hierarchy that controlled musicians' careers at that time. "Symphony No. 35" was written in 1782 for the Salzburg burgomeister's son, Siegmund Haffner. Mozart was met with apathy and malice from those who controlled his livelihood, and he endured jealousy from his rivals.

His character was accurately reflected in the stage play and movie "Amadeus." The enthusiasm of the "Presto" was a typical extension of Mozart's personality: fun-loving, affable, full of vitality. He sang, wrote music, and danced, fashioning new beauty into his music as he awaited the moment of fame and fortune that never again came in his lifetime.

If you like the enthusiastic feelings from this Mozart symphony, try Michael Gettel's "Fire from the Sky" from *The Art of Nature* (new age), BeauSoleil's "Jeunes Filles de Quatorze Ans" from La Danse de la Vie (zydeco), "Hallelujah Chorus" from Handel's the "Messiah" (classical), or Yanni's "Swept Away" from *Live at the Acropolis* (new age/jazz).

Now you have the basics, your core library. But since you are an individual, many pieces of music will speak to your individual condition, thus, in the next three chapters we'll expand the range of music you can adapt to any situation, at any time. Each of the chapters will focus on specific emotions and on an eclectic array of music pieces, often seemingly different from one another, yet evoking that same kind of emotion. Explore "Unsettling" (chapter 8), luxuriate in all that is "Soothing" (chapter 9), and revel in "Energizing" (chapter 10). This is your music, universally and personally.

8

Music That Unsettles

THE TWELVE MUSIC choices in this chapter offer you the possibility that any style of music might have the right combination of musi celements to evoke Unsettling emotions. Look first for the emotion that you want to match with music. You'll find music of varying moods within the Unsettled category: sadness, mournfulness, depression, anxiety, anger, and fear. Although you may disagree with the mood label as you listen to the music at different times, you may definitely hear Unsettled feelings in the music, and your inner self will respond. Remember, too, that Unsettling is not meant to be negative. It represents the emotions that confront us in life, emotions you need to face and acknowledge to deal with successfully.

The core music selections presented in this chapter and in Appendix A and B include rock, jazz, rap, blues, country, popular, classical, film, new age and soul. Other listening suggestions are listed at the end of each work. They are based on the music elements of that core music's mood and style. Music elements of other styles are then analyzed to give you the opportunity to shift to other degrees of Unsettling moods. Mixing styles is a good idea because it both liberates your ear and increases the USE potential of your music collection.

Sadness

MUSIC SELECTION: "The Thunder Rolls" (3:40) from
No Fences and *The Hits* (new country)
ARTIST: Garth Brooks
INSTRUMENTATION: Vocal, guitar, bass, drums, recorded nature sounds

Commentary: Crackling thunder opens this country music hit, which may make you feel a degree of gloominess as well as sadness. The guitar enters playing three notes that endlessly repeat, introducing these lyrics sung with bending notes that accentuate this mood. The bass, electric guitar, and drums enter later to emphasize intensifying anger.

Three-thirty in the morning, not a soul in sight
The city's like a ghost town, on a moonless summer night
Raindrops on the windshield, there's a storm moving in
He's headin' back from somewhere, that he never should have been

Every light is burnin' in a house across town
She's pacin' by the telephone, in her faded flannel gown
Askin' for a miracle, hopin' she's not right
Prayin' it's the weather that's kept him out all night

And the thunder rolls. . .And the thunder rolls

The thunder rolls and the lightin' strikes
Another love grows cold on a sleepless night
As the storm blows on, out of control
Deep in her heart, the thunder rolls

She's waitin' at the window as he pulls into the drive
She rushes out to hold him, thankful he's alive
But on the wind and rain, a brand new perfume blows
The lightin' flashes in her eyes, and he knows that she knows

And thunder rolls. . . and the thunder rolls

During the chorus repeats all instruments evoke an atmosphere of trouble brewing. The guitar makes one last plaintive wail as the band slowly exits, leaving crackling thunder and rain to fade out. The strength of the music and lyrics is enough to produce a safe Unsettled mood, whereas the video for this song adds visual elements which may evoke a destructive mood that I do *not* recommend matching.

If you find yourself responding to this mood, you might also consider the next selection, "I Seen a Man Die," as well as Boyz II Men's "Lonely Heart" from *Cooleyhighharmony* (R & B), "Adagio Lamentoso" from Tchaikovsky's "6-Pathetique" Symphony No. (classical), or Jan Garbarek and The Hilliard Ensemble's "Primo Tempore" from *Officium* (classical-Gregorian/jazz).

MUSIC SELECTION:	"I Seen a Man Die" (4:30) from *The Diary* (rap)
ARTIST:	Scarface
INSTRUMENTATION:	Master of Ceremonies, keyboard, guitar, bass, drums

Commentary: Depending on your "entrainment" factor with the anapestic beat, this song could make you feel a degree of agitation, or just plain sad. If instead you are feeling Energized by this music, listen to selections from chapter 10, to compare your response. The rap combination of repetitive, minimal musical sounds does not intensify emotions; the intensity is in the voice's frustration and in the lyrics.

"I Seen a Man Die" begins with a conversation about the plans of one young man just out of prison. Sustained high notes on the keyboard and low, two-note bass phrases continue this hopeful phase, which ends as the drum's anapestic beat (di-di-*DAH*) begins. The rapper's voice enters with the anapestic beat, stressing words that are important to the story line: *different, years, free.* The words string together thoughts of our social system's inability to transform this man either during or after imprisonment, because soon after his release he commits murder, returns to jail for thirty more years, and still feels pain because the system in unable to help him.

The chorus asks us to conceive of people reconciling their differences, to do what he exhorts, "you *see* the ones you never learned to *love* in life. Make the *change*, let it go. . .If you *ain't* at peace with God you need to *patch* it up." "I Seen a Man Die" suggests a process that may result in a cathartic release of sadness.

Another rap song that evokes a helpful sadness, although too close to depression for some, is 2 PAC's recent release "So Many Tears." Supporting the message of "I Seen a Man Die," "So Many Tears" communicates remorse from living a life that brought pain to self and others. Rap music and the trauma in the lives of those the songs concern is forcing the music industry to examine its responsibility to provide music that may or may not enhance health, but does not necessarily disturb it. Time Warner Inc. is a dramatic example of internal upheavals which have resulted in the emergence of a renewed responsibility toward public well-being.

The mood created by "I Seen a Man Die" can also be found in k.d. lang's "Outside Myself" (country), Josh White's and Robin Batteau's "House of the Rising Sun" (blues), "Pain Revisited" from Shara Nelson's *What Silence Knows* (popular), or the next selection, "Pearls."

Mournfulness

MUSIC SELECTION: "Pearls" (4:35) from *Best of Sade* (soul)
ARTIST: Sade
INSTRUMENTATION: Vocal, strings, guitar

Commentary: The lyrics match closely the elemental musical sadness in "Pearls," evoking moods that remain mournful. The lack of background drumbeat intensifies the lack of drive, the state of being trapped in listlessness.

Sade sings about a woman in Somalia who is dying as she tries to survive life, not knowing what motivates her to sustain life. For tension, the strings create a tremolo effect (the bow moves quickly, back and forth, across the string in one place). Then Sade and the cello fall into a slow call-response pattern.

The strings continue with low-pitched, sustained tones. Sade's voice has minimal vibrato, emphasizing the mournfulness. Then she starts crying a sorrowful, higher-pitched "Hallelujah" over the strings lower-pitched tremolo, and the strings increase in volume to meet the voice's intensity. Sade sings the woman's cries to

God about the world she doesn't want. The strings grow quiet and the cello plays a slow, solo melody. The guitar enters and Sade's slow improvisation of bending notes follows the cello's line and fades to an end.

For similar mood-matching music, try the next classical music selection, "Lento Sostenuto" from Gorecki's "Symphony No. 3," as well as Peter Gabriel's "Mercy Street" (rock), Counting Crows' "Perfect Blue Buildings" (alternative rock), or Amanda McBroom's "The Rose" (popular).

MUSIC SELECTION:	"Lento Sostenuto" (26:25) from "Symphony No. 3, Opus 36" (classical)
COMPOSER:	Henryck Gorecki
INSTRUMENTATION:	Full orchestra

Commentary: Neither Gorecki nor this symphony, composed in 1976, were widely known until this movement. "Lento Sostenuto" was featured in the 1993 movie "Fearless," starring Jeff Bridges as the survivor of an air crash. "Fearless" started the symphony on its march toward gold. The "Lento Sostenuto" movement was played at the end of the movie while Bridges chokes from an allergic reaction. Bridges has a near-death experience and relives the airplane crash in graphic intensity. For him, the sounds of the crash don't exist: no screams, no machine noises, no crashing, only the music. As the music continues, his wife desperately tries to resuscitate him.

The string bass section opens this music with extremely low, slow notes that divide into separate lines of melody, slowly ascending or descending in pitch. The volume gradually builds as the cellos join in, adding more melodic lines. The violas enter, then the violins, and eventually the range of notes and thickness of polyphony make the music sound like rich mud. This thickness slowly lightens, as polyphonic lines (the various instruments and melodic lines) are removed. The violins wind down from their high notes, the cellos drop out, and only violins and violas remain playing.

The piano enters, slowly repeating the same note to prepare for the female voice (soprano) as she begins to sing a fifteenth-century Polish lament by an unknown writer, who is addressing her cherished son.

The rest of the orchestra joins as her voice intensifies in sorrow, telling a story familiar to mothers over the centuries, when a son leaves. This mother's song recounts her faithful care of her son. She has always taken care of him, has always carried him in her heart. She pleads with him to make her happy now, to renew her hope for him.

The violins continue the singer's high melodic line above the rest of the orchestra. The eight separate lines of melody begin to diminish as each section of instruments again gradually drops out: Violins leave first, then violas, cellos, and finally the basses resolve the harmony with the last note.

If this music evokes a response within you, try the following music selections: "Perfect Blue Buildings" by Counting Crows (alternative rock), the Beatles "I Want You" from *Abbey Road*, Chopin's "Funeral March," or "Adagio Lamentoso" from Tchaikovsky's "Symphony No. 6" (both classical).

Depression

MUSIC SELECTION:	"Perfect Blue Buildings" (4:57) from *August and Everything After* (alternative rock)
ARTIST:	Counting Crows
INSTRUMENTATION:	Vocals, keyboards, organ, accordion, harmonica, electric guitar, electric bass, drums

Commentary: This alternative rock song is heavy with gloom as well as a degree of hopelessness. The drummer starts with a slow walking beat of 1-2-3-4 and never changes the tempo. The melancholy guitar enters soon after the drummer, always playing a syncopated beat. Equally melancholy keyboards play soft, sustained background harmonies. The male voice is mostly low-pitched, bending notes; he sounds close to crying.

The music's doom and gloom match the singer's desire to run away from himself, to fade into obscurity, recognizing that his life is at its lowest point. There is an instrumental interlude after the second chorus where the vocalist wails sustained higher notes, with all instruments playing louder, intensifying the emotional experience for the band and the listener. As the last strains are heard, the instruments fall away one by one until only the gloomy voice remains. The guitar drops out first, then the drummer leaves the keyboard playing soft background drones, and these too die as the voice slowly cries, confronted with his inability to escape from himself.

This CD won 1994 Album of the Year in alternative rock. The entire CD is "dark," and "Perfect Blue Buildings" specifically communicates this black, Unsettled mood. Other music to consider includes the following selections: Peter Gabriel's "Mercy Street" (rock), as well as country singer k.d. lang's "Outside Myself," Chopin's classical "Funeral March," or Jan Garbarek and The Hilliard Ensemble's "Primo Tempore" from *Officium* (classical-Gregorian/jazz).

MUSIC SELECTION: "Mercy Street" (4:43) from *So* (rock)
ARTIST: Peter Gabriel
INSTRUMENTATION: Vocals, keyboards, (processed) sax, surdu, congas, triangle, bass, drums

Commentary: Peter Gabriel fashions words with poetic essence; his lyrics are ambiguous. He dedicates this piece to poet Anne Sexton, who committed suicide. Likewise, her own poetry held undercurrents of uneasiness, tension, and melancholy as she explored issues of incest, abortion, drug addiction, and madness.

The keyboards begin moodily with sustained, mid-to-high range notes. The bass has several, separate sustained notes, each answered with a few notes from the keyboard. Over this is a steady percussion rhythm of bells, soon joined by syncopated drumbeats. Gabriel begins singing of empty streets which transform into visions that to him become real.

Mantra-like, the lyrics change to repeated words that portray sailing in a boat at night. The bass is in the background simulates a beating heart. Gabriel continues singing about visions in streets of mercy, portraying a naked soul who has visions of mercy within her father's arms.

The keyboard improvises a melody to introduce a confession of secrets to a priest, disturbing secrets that only a priest—here called the "doctor"—can bear. The same melody plays, then the voice enters from a distance calling and looking for mercy, which is echoed by guitar, keyboard, and other voices. Gabriel's voice sings the last lyrics, envisioning Anne sailing in a boat with her daddy, riding the ocean waves. The keyboard's bass note is the last thing you hear.

Other music selections similar in mood are alternative rock group Counting Crows' and the Beatles' rock selections herein, Chopin's "Funeral March," "Lento Sostenuto" from Gorecki's "Symphony No. 3" (both classical), or Josh White Jr. and Robin Batteau's "House of the Rising Sun" (blues).

MUSIC SELECTION: "I Want You (She's So Heavy)" (7:40) from *Abbey Road* (rock 'n' roll)
ARTIST: Beatles
INSTRUMENTATION: Vocals, keyboards, guitar, bass, drums

Commentary: The lyrics are simply, "I want you" and "she's so heavy," which are sung minimally, with the instruments controlling most of the song. This rock 'n' roll music is not the typical flavor of "rockin 'n' rollin" from the 1950s. It almost gives a hint of what's to come in rock: improvisation. But rather than experimenting with melody changes to create new feelings, here the "improv" becomes an endless dark duration of the same melody, harmony, rhythm, tempo, and intensity.

The rhythm guitar starts out with a solid, repetitive bass line and lead guitar wailing above. Then the lyrics enter with the lead guitar singing the melody with the words from the title "I Want You" over a punctuated rhythm by drums—DA-DA-DA. The band emphasizes being mad (or crazy) with a driving rhythm. The lyrics start to bemoan wanting somebody so badly that it drives one mad, and repeat, and repeat. . .

The words change to, "she's so heavy," followed by the former lyrics' melody played by the band, without vocals. The guitar repeats the melody countless times before "she's so heavy" comes in again with vocals. The two different melodies are constantly exchanged, driving the mood deeper down each time. Then, without any warning, the music stops abruptly. The absence of sound is a shock to the listener.

The mood created by this piece is also found in the two preceding pieces, Peter Gabriel's rock song "Mercy Street" and alternative rock group Counting Crows' "Perfect Blue Buildings." For similar moods, try country singers Garth Brooks' "The Thunder Rolls" and k.d. lang's "Outside Myself," Sade's "Pearls" (soul), or "I Seen a Man Die" from Scarface's *The Diary* (rap).

Anxiety

MUSIC SELECTION:	"Festival of Crows" (3:19) from *Poems of the Five Mountains* (new age)
ARTIST:	Timmerman and Wise
INSTRUMENTATION:	Keyboards, guitar, bass, drums

Commentary: The music opens with sharp, dissonant harmony and a call-response pattern between higher and lower dissonant patterns—crows cawing at one another. An anxious mood can set in quickly.

The tempo is fast throughout. The guitar enters with a slower melodic line that keeps pace with the cawing crows. Another keyboard line enters with a second melody, the bass comes in with intermittent sustained notes, then come the drums with conga sounds.

I don't know if crows always caw at the same volume, but the intensity of "Festival of Crows" never lets up; there are no soft or loud parts. The end is a final blast of dissonance.

To discover emotions similar to those in "Festival of Crows," listen to classical selections "Allegro" from Shostakovich's "Symphony No. 10," Janacek's "Sinfonietta," and Wagner's "Ride of the Valkyries," or rock group Gwen Mars' "Heal Me."

MUSIC SELECTION:	"Infernal Dance" (4:14) from "Firebird Suite, Part I" (classical)
COMPOSER:	Igor Stravinsky (1882–1971)
INSTRUMENTATION:	Full orchestra

Commentary: Visualize the wild Fire Bird performing a whirlwind dance in his enchanted orchard before the Prince enters, or visualize any defiant wild creature's anxiety as man approaches.

The movement opens with a short, strident symphonic chord

that is repeated sporadically. The woodwinds take over the theme with strings actively pursuing them with "pizzicato" (plucking their strings) rhythms and bell-sound accents. A second theme is announced between the violins and woodwinds. The brass take over, announcing again the first theme. The dissonant harmonies produce unrelenting cacophony.

The brass dominate, now pushing through with regular, driving beats, punctuated by the tympani. Solo instruments begin tossing themes around until the tympani climaxes this section.

The volume drops suddenly, so you hear the strings emphatically plucking one theme as the percussion section maintains separate, erratic rhythms. The intensity climaxes once again and the instruments continue like whirling dervishes. With a last large swell of energy, two dramatic, successive crescendos hurry the entire orchestra to its final peak.

If this work resonates with you, explore similar feelings with pop singer Shara Nelson's "Pain Revisited," Berlioz's "Dream of a Sabbath Night" (classical), or the soundtracks "Betrayal and Desolation" from the film "Braveheart," and "Pruit Igoe" from "Koyaanisqatsi."

Anger

MUSIC SELECTION:	"Wings of Karma" (6:06) from *Apocalypse* (jazz/rock)
ARTIST:	Mahavishnu Orchestra
INSTRUMENTATION:	Band: electric violins, viola, cello, keyboards, guitars, bass, drums, percussion; London Symphony Orchestra

Commentary: Self-named Maha (the creator) Vishnu (the preserver), John McLaughlin creates an intensity that ignites irritation and agitation. This 1974 jazz-rock recording was McLaughlin's last and is considered a total expression of his thirty-two-year musical life.

The cellos start "Wings of Karma" with sustained low pitches. "The nasally oriental oboe snaking through the beginning"[1] is interrupted with brass notes, occasional drumbeats, and shimmering higher strings. The strings take over the melody as the orchestra slowly enters. Textures are constantly thinning and thickening, the dynamics (volume) constantly changing.

The jazz band enters with a fairly steady but jagged drumbeat. In solo improvisations, Mahavishnu (McLaughlin), on electric guitar, bends notes, then speeds up to run all over the instrument. His improv is topped by an even wilder electric violin as the orchestra repeats the syncopated rhythmic pattern.

Suddenly the jazz band fades, leaving only the orchestra's lower strings sustained notes. These are intermittent fast swells by the orchestra. A violin solo starts but is interrupted by the orchestra, which swells, quickly decrescendos, and then slowly fades out to the end.

A study completed by Florida State University researchers measured how long people would stay "on hold" until a counselor could assist them on the State of Florida Abuse Hot line. The study showed that jazz music kept callers "on hold" longer than classical, country, popular, or easy listening styles. "Wings of Karma" was one piece that promoted the *least* amount of telephone disconnections. It matched callers' moods while they were on hold: agitation.[2]

To find moods similar to "Wings of Karma," try rock group Gwen Mars' "Heal Me," Stravinsky's "Rite of Spring, Part I," or Berlioz's "Dream of a Sabbath Night" (both classical), or "Sinfonietta" by Janacek (classical).

MUSIC SELECTION: "Dream of a Sabbath Night" (9:00) from "Symphonie Fantastique" (classical)
COMPOSER: Hector Berlioz (1803–1869)
INSTRUMENTATION: Full orchestra

Commentary: Berlioz visually described the scene set by this movement: "Now he (the hero) sees himself in a frightful company—ghosts, magicians, monsters. . .Briefly he hears the melody (representing his beloved), but it is transformed, vulgar, grotesque. . . She joins him in the infernal orgy."[3] The mood effect becomes agitating and irritating as the music progresses to the end.

The bass and tympani enter quietly with four low notes. Strings and woodwinds follow with short melodic phrases. The violins shimmer in the background while the lower strings and brass continue to growl out the rhythm. The clarinet comes in with a distracting singsong melody, and the orchestra responds with dramatic, bombarding tympani.

The clarinet and strings come back with the singsong melody. The rest of the orchestra plays staccato (short) bursts that climax, then decrease, and a solo bassoon line introduces solo chimes. Other instruments interrupt with quick phrases that are squelched by the tympani.

The lower strings, woodwinds, and brass introduce the beauty-into-ghoul transformation theme that growls as it grows, offset by wild rhythmic interludes. Continually, the instrument sections interrupt each other. The symphony races to the finish, incessantly repeating the rhythm. The "infernal orgy" finally halts when the brass section explodes into a piercing sustained C-note.

Many of the same feelings can be evoked with the following classical music selections: "Allegro" from Shostakovich's "Symphony No. 10," as well as "Pruit Igoe" from the soundtrack of "Koyaanisqatsi," "The Battle on the Ice" from the film "Alexander Nevsky" and "Mars, Bringer of War" from Holst's "The Planets" (both classical).

Fear

MUSIC SELECTION: "Allegro" (4:10) from "Symphony No. 10 in E minor" (classical)
COMPOSER: Dmitri Shostakovich (1906–1975)
INSTRUMENTATION: Full orchestra

Commentary: This dark-colored symphony was composed during the summer of 1953, within months of Stalin's death. Stalin had forbidden this kind of music in Russia because it allowed too much intense human emotion.

The second movement, "Allegro," represents the terror that prevailed during the Stalinist regime. Although it is the shortest movement, its speed is so fierce and driving that it stands in sharp contrast to the other movements.

"Allegro" opens with strings playing low and brusque rhythms before the woodwinds bring in the theme. Quick, decisive percussion (snare drum rolls initially) begin to punctuate the woodwinds' melody. Led by the strings, the whole orchestra joins in, with the woodwinds adding high piccolo trills. The strings and woodwinds exchange the theme as the percussion revolves around them. Fierce driving beats take over among the brass, woodwinds, and strings.

The brass start a slower but still driving beat with a new melody, as the rest of the symphony keeps the original rhythm. The brass drop out as the strings quietly continue playing. Gradually the volume builds again and the entire orchestra joins in at maximum volume, driving the fierce rhythm patterns to the end.

If Shostakovich's "Allegro" resonates with you, also consider Berlioz's "Dream of a Sabbath Night" or Janacek's "Sinfonietta" (both classical), Timmerman and Wise's "Festival of Crows" (new age), or Shara Nelson's "Pain Revisited" (popular).

Unwelcome emotions are a fact of life. There are many ways to deal with them, but repressing them and hoping they'll go away are among the worst. Getting in touch with those emotions through music is a gentle start toward healing them, or rather, healing yourself. Your next step will be to find a Soothing respite and the music to take you there.

9

Music That Soothes

THE SOOTHING MUSIC you are looking for is found in various moods: tenderness, sentimentality, serenity, calmness, tranquility, and relaxation. The moods I have identified for each music selection act as guides only; your reaction may be slightly different. The styles in this chapter and in Appendix A and B include classical, country, Christian, jazz, rock, stage, film, opera, easy listening, new age, and world music. Other listening suggestions are given, which follow the same guidelines discussed in the preceding chapter. All have been chosen to help you find relaxation, serenity, and the peaceful places of your soul.

Sentimentality

MUSIC SELECTION:	"Sentimental" (6:34) from *Breathless* (jazz)
ARTIST:	Kenny G
INSTRUMENTATION:	Soprano saxophone, keyboards, guitar, synthesized bass, and drums

Commentary: Kenny G considers that not just every song but every note on this soft jazz recording was heartfelt and inspired. "These feelings only happen when they are ready. It is not something that any one person can dictate as the music is much bigger than the man. . . .My heart, soul, and two years of my life have gone into this collection of songs."[1] The artist's mother died during this period, which has to have added to the emotional content of the music.

"Sentimental" begins with the keyboard introducing a brief melody in a tempo that closely matches the heart at rest. Kenny G's mellow saxophone joins the keyboard, expanding the melody. Glide along with him, this suggests. When the saxophone repeats the melody, the bass begins emphasizing the first and third beats (*1*-2-*3*-4). The drums and percussion enter on beats 1-*2*-3-*4* so the combined sound is evenly accented, which makes the rhythm feel very regular. The soothing improvisations continue to reach higher and lower. Nearing the end, drums, percussion, and bass fade out, leaving the saxophone and keyboards to sustain the last lower, soft notes.

If you find yourself in the mood Kenny G created, try also Kostia and David Arkenstone's "The Cello's Song," the "Ballad Theme" from Gershwin's "Rhapsody in Blue" (classical/jazz), "Chant" (classical-Gregorian), and "Unforgettable," an easy listening song, explained in detail next.

Music Selection:	"Unforgettable" (3:29) from *Unforgettable* (easy listening)
Artist:	Natalie Cole, duo with Nat King Cole (1917–1965)
Instrumentation:	Vocals, strings, piano, guitar, bass, drums

Commentary: First recorded in 1951 by Nat King Cole, the "Unforgettable" experience is relived every time Natalie performs the song. Her dad's voice is on tape as they sing together. You can feel the nostalgia within the music's tenderness.

The piano opens with slow, regular bass and drumbeats leading into Nat's voice, with Natalie echoing his words. The timbre of their voices are closely matched—length of vibrato, silky velvet tones. Their words inspire you to reminisce about someone special. The strings hover above their pitch to highlight the sentimental lyrics, and add texture throughout the song. As the blended voices of father and daughter sing words that marvel at such an extraordinary relationship that spurs mutual admiration, the strings swell with saxophone and piano to sustain the last notes.

For similar mood-matching music, USE Puccini's aria "O mio babbino caro" from "Gianni Schicchi" (opera), as well as Liszt's "Liebestraum No. 3" (classical), Christian trumpeter Phil Driscoll's "I've Just Seen Jesus," and the next stage selection, "The Music of the Night."

Tenderness

MUSIC SELECTION:	"The Music of the Night" (5:05) from "Phantom of the Opera" (stage)
MUSIC/LYRICS:	Andrew Lloyd Webber/Charles Hart and Richard Stilgoe
INSTRUMENTATION:	Male vocal, orchestra

Commentary: As the music begins, the voice also begins falling and rising, the words entreating you to follow him. "Nighttime sharpens, heightens each sensation. Darkness stirs and wakes imagination. . .Silently the senses abandon their defences." The orchestra stays out of the way, accompanying in very low, sustained notes until the cellos and woodwinds finish the singer's melody.

The singer continues, "Slowly, gently night unfurls its splendour. Grasp it, sense it—tremulous and tender. . .Turn your face away from the garish light of day. Turn your thoughts away from cold, unfeeling light—and listen to the music of the night. . ." The orchestra swells to make you want to "close your eyes and surrender to your darkest dreams! Purge your thoughts of the life you knew before! Close your eyes, let your spirit start to soar!" The orchestra leaves as the singer holds that soaring high note, disappearing so that you concentrate on his words, "And you'll live as you've never lived before. . ."

The words are evocative of the compelling melody: "Softly, deftly, music shall caress you. . .Hear it, feel it, secretly possess you. . . " The orchestra crescendos with the horns to emphasize, "Let your mind start a journey through a strange new world! Leave all thoughts of the world you knew before! Let your soul take you where you long to be!" This climax is followed by silence, then the singer softly suggests, "Only then can you belong to me. . ." This piece can silence a roomful of chattering people and enwrap the single listener, as the seductive vocals and the ebb and swell of the orchestra accentuate "the power of the music of the night."

To discover emotions similar to "The Music of the Night," listen to Trisha Yearwood's country song "You Can Sleep While I Drive," the "Ballad Theme" from George Gershwin's "Rhapsody in Blue" (classical/jazz), Kenny G's saxophone solo in "Sentimental" (jazz), and the next selection, "Evergreen."

MUSIC SELECTION:	"Evergreen" (3:00) from "A Star is Born" (film)
ARTIST:	Barbra Streisand
INSTRUMENTATION:	Vocal, piano, guitar

Commentary: The meaning of "Evergreen's" lyrics closely matches what the music elements communicate: loving tenderness. Soft guitar sets the tempo beneath the high voice. The piano answers the voice and then the lyrics picture a love that embraces like a comfortable chair in the fresh morning air. The bass and faint drum give the feeling of security, playing a constant, regular rhythm as the singer celebrates the certainty of love just found.

Streisand has the vocal fluidity to melt notes together without separating them, varying the vibrato and elegantly enunciating words. She is justly famed for her ability to sustain final notes, which holds true for her last words that describe time's everlasting love that is "evergreen."

Many of the same feelings can be evoked with the following music: "O mio babbino caro" from the opera "Gianni Schicchi," country singer Trisha Yearwood's "You Can Sleep While I Drive," Mike Rowland's new age *Fairy Ring*, and the following piece, "Mysterious Island."

Calmness

MUSIC SELECTION:	"Mysterious Island" (5:49) from *Planet Drum* (new age/world)

ARTIST: Mickey Hart
INSTRUMENTATION: Grand dumbec, body percussion, bird
                     whistles, nose flute, tambourine, wind
                     chimes, seagulls, vocals, udu drum

Commentary: Jungle sounds of water, birds, rain, and blowing
wind create a soothing background for the consistent percussion
rhythms. Bells start mirroring bird whistles. The human voice sustains mid-range pitches, without words, as a flute calls in the
background. The thick texture of layered sounds is balanced and
soothing. The consistent tempo allows the heart to beat in a state
of rest.

   Mickey Hart, drummer with the Grateful Dead, is an advocate
of world music and music therapy, and is highly respected by fellow drummers for integrating world percussion instruments,
some very rare, in ways that blend a new music. When he testified
before the U. S. Senate in support of music therapy, Hart affirmed
his belief that "rhythm is at the center of our lives. By acknowl-
edging this fact and acting on it, our potential for preventing illness and maintaining mental, physical, and spiritual well-being is
far greater. . . .It is the connection with these rhythms that gives
music the power to heal."[2]

   If you find yourself resonating with this mood, consider a new
age selection, "Foglute" from *Isle of Skye*, "Clair de Lune" by
Debussy (classical), "Cool Mountain Stream" (new age-environmental) and the next music selection, "Fantasia on Greensleeves"
(classical).

MUSIC SELECTION: "Fantasia on Greensleeves" (4:41)
                     (classical)
COMPOSER: Ralph Vaughan Williams (1872–1958)
INSTRUMENTATION: Orchestra

Commentary: The flute begins with high notes playing the solo
introduction with harp accompaniment. Opening with this thin
texture, plus the gentle familiarity of the piece, hooks you into the
music.

   The harp slowly strumming at the heart-at-rest tempo of 60
bpm introduces the rest of the strings which play the

"Greensleeves" melody. Then the violins play a higher-pitched tremolo (trembling bow) that takes the melody into variations of cellos and violas, then flute, and finally violins. The flute solo heard at the beginning is repeated, the harp strumming on the beat, a very slow 1-2-3-4. The cellos and violins join with the harp to carry the Soothing melody to the last note.

In Shakespeare's "The Merry Wives of Windsor" Sir John Falstaff says, "Let the sky. . .thunder to the tune of Green Sleeves."[3] Initially played as roistering music, the melody was first published in 1652, and music folklore says Queen Elizabeth I composed it. Vaughan Williams transformed "Greensleeves" into its current wishfulness, using it in "The Merry Wives" (1912) at Stratford-on-Avon in England and in his opera "Sir John in Love" (1929). Today there are many different recordings of "Greensleeves" available, including those by Steven Halpern (new age—*Timeless*) and the Boston Pops Orchestra (classical—*Pops in Love*).

For other selections that evoke a similar calming mood, try the classical piece "The Lark Ascending," also by Vaughan Williams, Jean Michel Jarre's *Equinox* (new age), Pachelbel's classical "Canon," or James Galway's "Song of the Seashore" (new age/world).

MUSIC SELECTION:	"Forever" (11:14) from *The Edge of Forever* (new age)
ARTIST:	Hilary Stagg
Instrumentation:	Electrified harp, keyboard synthesizers, flute, vocals

Commentary: Ocean waves begin "Forever," followed by sustained bass notes, bells, and harp. The flute complements the harp's melodies as synthesized strings enter. The texture is thick with layers of sound as both sustained notes and melody lines are exchanged between instruments. Synthesized voices follow the flute line. The bass continues throughout with soft beats on *1-2-3-4*.

An unusual element here is the silence: Brief pauses allow you to refocus on the music. Throughout, all sounds are evenly balanced, raising no irritation, but evoking, hopefully, your own even balance. Near the end, all instruments fade out, leaving only the ocean waves, which eventually fade as well.

I was fascinated by the three-panel artwork within *The Edge of Forever* CD. Colors of purple, teal, rose, gold, white, and blue accent tunnel clouds explored by rainbow-colored nymphs. The colors and movement capture the essence of the music, a goal for which many cover designs aim, but few do as well. Try looking at it while you listen to the music, as a form of art and music therapy combined.

Other works that produce similar feelings include new age selections *Fairy Ring* by Mike Rowland and "Cool Mountain Stream" by Platinum Disc Corp., as well as classical pieces such as Liszt's "Liebestraum No. 3" and "Largo" from "Winter" of Vivaldi's "The Four Seasons."

Tranquility

MUSIC SELECTION: *Chant* (57:36) (classical-Gregorian)
ARTIST: The Benedictine Monks of Santo
                    Domingo de Silos
INSTRUMENTATION: Vocals

Commentary: The entire recording is a compilation of Gregorian chants sung by monks at the Monastery of Santo Domingo de Silos in Spain. The Latin text comes from Roman Catholic Church liturgy and is sung in unison as a single melodic line, "free of rhythm, soaring into space with a calm certainty that is magical."[4]

There have been many recordings of Gregorian chants, but this one seems magical, attracting people of all ages and music preferences. Chants help many people focus on a task—whether it is working on the computer, reading, or meditating. There are midrange pitches; a slow, unobtrusive melody; a thin texture; pleasing harmonies; long durations; haunting vocal timbres; slower vibratos; no rhythm to energize you; and because the lyrics are in Latin, you probably won't be straining to listen to the words.

If you like the tranquility of *Chant*, consider also Jean Michel Jarre's *Equinox* (new age), trance rock-style Autechre's "Windwind," "Adagio" from Saint-Saens' "Organ Symphony in C# minor" (classical), or the following selection, "Healing Dance" (new age/world).

MUSIC SELECTION:	"Healing Dance" (9:14) from *Music to Disappear in II* (new age/world)
ARTIST:	Raphael
INSTRUMENTATION:	Piano, keyboards, violin, flutes, bansuri, drums, percussion

Commentary: "Healing Dance" begins with a thin texture: one violin in a slow, dreamy, fluid solo. Then the percussion section establishes the rhythm, a steady 1-2-3-4 that matches the heart beat at rest. The violin and bansuri (oriental instrument) enter separately and begin a call-response pattern. The flute also enters to create and complement melody lines. Near the end of "Healing Dance" the sound of ocean waves is slightly evident, loud enough to promote a soothing effect but not to command your attention. The end is a slow fade of all sounds.

Other songs on this recording feature the Australian didgeridoo, harp, and wordless vocals (sustained vowel sounds). If you find yourself moved by "Healing Dance," try listening to classical composer Smetana's "The Moldau," Kostia and David Arkenstone's "The Cello's Song" (new age), or Gershwin's classical/jazz "Ballad Theme" from "Rhapsody in Blue."

Relaxation

MUSIC SELECTION:	"Largo" (2:30) from "Winter" of "The Four Seasons" (classical)
COMPOSER:	Antonio Vivaldi (1678–1741)
INSTRUMENTATION:	Violins, violas, cellos, harpsichord

Commentary: A solo violin plays an easy-to-remember melody throughout "Largo." The harpsichord and the rest of the strings accompany the solo violin in a regular rhythmic pattern (1-2-3-4). Every beat is stressed the same, and the tempo is 60 bpm, the heart at rest. "Largo" is one of fifty-seven Baroque selections that was chosen out of 400 possibilities by The LIND (Learning in New Dimensions) Institute. The Institute's research indicated that music from the Baroque era is the most conducive to bringing about the state of relaxation necessary to retain learning information within long-term memory.

The best tempo to help you relax is between 55-70 bpm. When shopping for a recording of Vivaldi's "Largo," for optimum relaxation, look at the insert to confirm the length of the piece: it should be approximately two minutes and thirty seconds. If the recording indicated is shorter, "Largo" was played too fast. You may still feel mellow, but you won't experience total relaxation. Two other LIND Institute Baroque selections are Haydn's "Adagio Cantabile" (optimally 3:04) and Gluck's "Minuet from Orpheus and Eurydice" (6:40 is recommended).

For music considerations that evoke a similar mood to "Largo," you might also try classical composers Handel's "Water Music" or Pachelbel's "Canon," Windham Hill artist George Winston's "Autumn" (new age), or the next selection, "Song of the Seashore."

MUSIC SELECTION:	"Song of the Seashore" (3:40) from *Song of the Seashore and other Melodies of Japan* (new age/world)
COMPOSER:	Narita
INSTRUMENTATION:	Flute, string orchestra, harp, koto

Commentary: I thought I heard a bit of "The Shadow of Your Smile" in the flute solo that opens this song, but the cumulative effect of this gentle piece is very Japanese, very Zen. Very slow and fluid throughout, in relaxing mid-range pitches, the harp and strings support the flute's melody. The cellos and violins also take turns carrying the melody, changing the range of pitches from high to low. At the end, the flute holds the melody, joined by a solo violin, then a light touch of strings for the final sustained note.

Considerable research has been done on prenatal music, music for mothers-to-be and their babies. This particular selection, recorded in Tokyo by James Galway and the Tokyo String Orchestra, is recommended for relaxation.[5]

If you like the relaxing feelings of "Song of the Seashore," try Japan-based new age artist Kitaro's *Light of the Spirit*, Hilary Stagg's "Forever" (new age), the theme from the soundtrack of the film "Chariots of Fire" by Vangelis, or Debussy's "Clair de Lune."

MUSIC SELECTION: "Fogflute" (3:00) from *Isle of Skye*
                         (new age)
COMPOSER: Jeffrey Thompson, D.C.
INSTRUMENTATION: Synthesizers

Commentary: I call Dr. Thompson's music "harmonic entrainment" recordings. He has designed specific frequencies within the range of alpha and theta brain wave patterns to help move you into deep relaxation while listening to *Isle of Skye*. Used for hypnosis worldwide, *Isle of Skye* has received the highest recommendation by the National Hypnotherapy Association.

"Fogflute" is one of twelve different music selections on this recording. It begins with low flute sounds repeating a slow melody with barely discernible vibrato. There is no rhythm and no other instrument timbres; synthesized rain falls throughout the music.

If you discovered relaxation with "Fogflute," I suggest you try Thompson's *Egg of Time* (new age) as well as these new age selections: Mickey Hart's "Mysterious Island" and "Cool Mountain Stream" from the *Relaxation* series; or Bach's "Air on the G String" (classical).

> **Note:** Did you discover music that lies in the "gray" area for you, in between Soothing-Energized or Soothing-Unsettled? This gray-area music may be very USEful to you when you match your mood with music in a sequence. Next we'll review the music that takes you into the soaring realm of Energy.

10

Music That Energizes

THESE MUSIC SELECTIONS may be so Energizing that you can still USE them without sequencing and be energized. That charges the battery but doesn't fix the engine. If quick energy is what you want, this is your music. If long-term energy levels are what you need, this music is part of the process. Just as excitement can mask fear or anxiety, people can experience Unsettling music—which provokes moods such as anger, anxiety, or fear—by feeling excitement. Here is a general guideline to the mix of music elements that may separate these kinds of Unsettling moods from the Energizing ones.

Anxiety or Fear (Unsettled) music elements: Very fast tempos; many notes (pitches) played very quickly, which move over a wide range of high-to-low pitches; instruments interrupting one another.

Excitement (Energizing) music elements: Fast tempos; dancing rhythms; memorable melodies; timbres (instruments) that sound pleasing, with their intensities balanced for positive energy.

The Energizing music styles presented in this chapter (and in Appendix A and B) include country, zydeco, gospel, jazz, rock, popular, film, classical, opera, new age, and world. Any one of these music styles might have the right combination of music elements to evoke Energizing emotions. Expand your horizons to consider music you wouldn't have thought of previously to help you achieve the energy level for which you're looking.

Exhilaration

MUSIC SELECTION:	"Let the Beat Control Your Body" (3:38) from *No Limits* (techno rock)
ARTIST:	2 Unlimited
INSTRUMENTATION:	Vocal, electronic

Commentary: This techno rock song includes computerized sounds which simulate a variety of live instruments. It begins with a fast-paced presto tempo of Brazilian rhythms, played by a few single-tone percussion instruments, and quickly expanding to full percussion. The melody line enters in a series of quick organ chords over the Brazilian rhythms. A fast-moving bass line enters, which adds yet another dimension of texture that hooks you further into the music. Occasional voices punctuate the flow of high energy. "I want you to let the beat control your body...when you let it penetrate your brain." Other drum sounds enter (trashcan lids?) to keep the action interesting.

If you are driving long distances and concerned about falling asleep, techno rock, in general, and this piece, in particular, is a definite energy source. If you find yourself responding positively to "Let the Beat Control Your Body," try listening to the Clark Sisters' "Hallelujah" from *Black Gospel Explosion*, Herbie Hancock's "Dis Is Da Drum" (jazz), BeauSoleil's "Jeunes Filles de Quatorze Ans" (zydeco), or the following selection, "Orange Blossom Special."

MUSIC SELECTION:	"Orange Blossom Special" (5:30) from *The New Nashville Cats* (country)
ARTIST:	Mark O'Connor

INSTRUMENTATION: Fiddle, harmonicas, piano, keyboard synthesizers, electric and acoustic guitar, bass, drums

Commentary: Mark O'Connor is a legendary fiddle player who has been heard on more than 450 recordings. His special arrangement here has four tunes added to the "Orange Blossom Special": Bach's "Partita in E major," themes from "Bonanza" and "The Flintstones," as well as Tchaikovsky's "Nutcracker Suite." O'Connor's style truly communicates infectious exhilaration.

The bass begins with a fast 1-2-3-4. The drums and harmonicas join in quickly, with the fiddle playing the locomotive whistle sounds. The texture never changes: all instruments remain to the end. The fiddler slides his fingers and bow around quickly, country-style, and yet cleanly, classical-style. The music is nonstop liveliness.

If you find your toe tapping to "Orange Blossom Special," you might try O'Connor's "New Country" from *Heroes*, as well as Sousa's "Stars and Stripes Forever," Mozart's "Presto" from "Symphony No. 35" (both classical), or Yanni's "Swept Away" (new age/jazz).

Cheerfulness

MUSIC SELECTION: "Practice Makes Perfect" (4:55) from *Dragonfly Summer* (jazz)
ARTIST: Michael Franks
INSTRUMENTATION: Vocal, keyboards, alto saxophone, guitar, bass, drums, percussion

Commentary: Drums start the mood right away with an anapestic rhythm. The guitar, bass, and keyboards begin immediately, each picking a rhythmic pattern that fills out the beats. Franks starts singing the melody which jumps around, sometimes flowing, sometimes changing quickly, in a jazz rhythm: " . . .I have heard it said 'nothing is perfect.' How untrue! Perfection's me and you. Practice makes perfect sense when it comes to love. . ."

Backup singers sustain "love" in the chorus, and the saxophone improvises between verses. Franks ends with "the look that's in your eyes convinces me it's time to practice" as the band keeps up the rhythmic tempo and the volume fades.

For similar mood-matching music, try listening to Bob Marley's "Soul Shakedown Party" from *At His Best* (reggae rock), "La donna e mobile" from Verdi's "Rigoletto" (opera), Enya's "Orinoco Flow," or Ray Lynch's "Celestial Soda Pop" from *Deep Breakfast* (both new age).

MUSIC SELECTION:	"In the Mood" (3:32) (jazz-big band)
ARTIST:	Glenn Miller
INSTRUMENTATION:	Saxophones, trumpets, trombones, bass, piano, percussion, drum set (or drum kit)

Commentary: This big band tune is infectious and cheery. The saxophones open the song with the catchy tune. Snatched by the trumpets, the melody is returned to the saxophones when the rhythm kicks in. The straightforward beat of 1-2-3-4 continues throughout the song, which entrains the heart rate easily.

The swing style of "In the Mood" is syncopated (accents between beats) by the saxophones, with the trumpets answering the saxes in a call-response pattern. The bass player's straight rhythms match the drums, then individual instruments start improvising: saxophone, trumpet. The trumpets declare 'the end' with a short ascending fanfare, which the saxophones sustain and the drums finish with a single hit.

Many swing socials lead off with this song because it gets everyone in the dancing mood. It's almost impossible to resist tapping your toes. If you like "In the Mood," consider also Chabrier's "Espana," "On the Beautiful Blue Danube" by Strauss (both classical), Joplin's "The Entertainer" (jazz-ragtime), or the next selection, "Brazil."

MUSIC SELECTION:	"Brazil"(3:22) from *Fiesta* (world)
COMPOSER:	Ary Barroso
ARTIST:	Cincinnati Pops Orchestra
INSTRUMENTATION:	Full orchestra

Commentary: "Brazil" begins with the sound of cowbells—cowbells in a syncopated rhythm, then maracas and drums joining in to fill out the samba rhythm. All instruments ask your body to move with the music. The brass match the percussion in a rhythmic fanfare, and the easy-to-remember melody enters with the strings and trumpet.

The orchestra softens, although the rhythm continues, to introduce a second melody played by the strings. When the brass continue to punctuate rhythmic patterns, taking the melody from the strings, the strings react with yet another melody, then leave the cowbells to start all over again. The full orchestra quickly joins in to crescendo to the final note.

"Brazil" was composed in 1939. Other outstanding performances of "Brazil" include those of Johnny Mathis and Dionne Warwick.

If you find yourself moving to "Brazil," you might also like "Just One World" from Craig Chaquico's *Acoustic Planet* (new age/new country), Ray Lynch's "Celestial Soda Pop" (new age), two lively opera arias, "La donna e mobile" from Verdi's "Rigoletto" and Bizet's "Votre toast (Toreador Song)" from "Carmen," or Elton John's "The Circle of Life" from the soundtrack of "The Lion King" film.

Joyousness

MUSIC SELECTION:	"Odessa" (3:32) from *The Sacred Fire* (new age)
COMPOSER/ARTIST:	Nicholas Gunn
INSTRUMENTATION:	Flutes, percussion, piano, synthesizers, vocals

Commentary: The flute announces the start of a tribal dance and the drums surround the straight 1-2-3-4 beats with syncopation. The flute continues on its path of sheer joy, backed by synthesized strings and keyboard, with male vocals joining intermittently. The rhythms are intense, but light: Everything focuses on the desire to dance.

If "Odessa" brings out the right energy for you, you might also try "Fire from the Sky" from Michael Gettel's *The Art of Nature* (new age), Herbie Hancock's "Dis Is Da Drum" (jazz), Sousa's "Stars and Stripes Forever" (classical), or the following selection, "Hallelujah Chorus."

MUSIC SELECTION: "Hallelujah Chorus" (3:55) from the "Messiah" (classical)

COMPOSER: George Frederick Handel (1685–1759)

INSTRUMENTATION: Chorus, full orchestra

Commentary: This music immediately asserts regal triumph, as the orchestra sets the musical pace (fast walking) and the chorus responds enthusiastically. The amount of instruments and choir members varies, depending upon the size of the concert hall or the number of volunteers for the church choir. The power of dozens of voices sung at maximum volume with the support of the orchestra is overwhelming.

Polyphony (thick texture) builds within the chorus as the basses begin, "And He shall reign forever and ever," continuing on while the tenors start the same phrase, then the altos, and finally the sopranos. The polyphony transitions then take on a call-response pattern:

The women sing, "King of Kings. . ." to which the men reply, ". . .Forever and ever. Hallelujah! Hallelujah!" "And Lord of Lords. . ." ". . .Forever and ever. Hallelujah! Hallelujah!" This repeats several times as the chorus ascends in pitch. Then the whole section, starting with "He shall reign. . .," continues over and over, repeating the fervor and energy up to the last sustained "Hallelujah!"

For similar mood-matching joy, consider "Hallelujah" from the Clark Sister's *Black Gospel Explosion*, BeauSoleil's "Jeunes Filles de Quatorze Ans" (zydeco), "Presto" from Mozart's "Symphony No. 35," or "Presto" from Beethoven's "Symphony No. 7" (both classical).

Lightheartedness

MUSIC SELECTION: "The Circle of Life" (3:50) from "The Lion King" (film)

COMPOSER/LYRICIST: Elton John/Tim Rice

INSTRUMENTATION: Vocals, drums, nature, synthesizers

Commentary: "The Circle of Life" can be classified as world music and leads off a wonderful soundtrack (it was number one on the charts for weeks) to a highly emotional film. It's the combination of the walking tempo and the light rhythm beneath the melodic line that creates the lighthearted, happy mood.

The song begins with jungle bird sounds, followed by male voices in the rhythmic call-response patterns of African chants, gradually accompanied by syncopated drumming. A solo voice begins the story: the cub's (or a child's) arrival the first day on this planet is overwhelming. When you see the sun, you realize what can be seen and done, and that life is full of possibilities.

The background chants continue with drumming as the solo voice intensifies with the chorus. The lyrics interpret the circle of life as a movement through discouragement and desire, trust and love, as one discovers his/her true purpose within that circle. The singing diminishes to a background lull as the film's visual images take over (lion cub baptism). The music crescendos on top of enthusiastic sounds from animals, then *boom!*, a loud drumbeat finishes the song.

I've been told more than once by parents who have taken their children to see "The Lion King" that "The Circle of Life" evokes some sadness now, because they know the storyline so well. Other songs from "The Lion King" soundtrack that are cheerful treasures for children include "Hakuna Matata" and "I Just Can't Wait to be King."

An adult looking for similar feelings of lightheartedness might try Enya's "Orinoco Flow" (new age), "Soul Shakedown Party" from Bob Marley's *At His Best* (reggae rock), Herbie Hancock's "Dis Is Da Drum" (jazz), or the next selection, "On the Beautiful Blue Danube" (classical).

MUSIC SELECTION:	"On the Beautiful Blue Danube" (10:00) (classical)
COMPOSER:	Johann Strauss (1825–1899)
INSTRUMENTATION:	Full orchestra

Commentary: "The Blue Danube" also begins slowly to warm your mood into one of lightheartedness. After the slow introduction there are five waltz sections, plus the ending, with each section a bit different, but all flowing smoothly from one to the next. Depending on the recording, the tempo will either remain consistent throughout, for dancing, or will vary slightly. This alters the degree of mood.

For instance, if "The Blue Danube" waltz were played at a faster tempo, it might produce more exhilaration for you. Played more slowly it could actually be Soothing (or irritating, if you're used to feeling it faster!).

The rhythm is *1*-2-3, with the stress on the first beat. It is easy to imagine yourself swaying and whirling to this beat, but even if you wouldn't be caught dead dancing a waltz, the lilting tempos may uplift your mood into one of cheerfulness.

You might also enjoy the positive energies in Scott Joplin's "The Entertainer" (jazz-ragtime), "Just One World" from Craig Chaquico's *Acoustic Planet* (new age/new country), Michael Franks' "Practice Makes Perfect" (jazz), or Chabrier's "Espana" (classical).

Enthusiasm

Music Selection:	"Emotions" (4:07) from *Emotions* (popular)
Artist:	Mariah Carey
Instrumentation:	Vocals, keyboards, drums

Commentary: The synthesizer creates an amazingly thick texture with a synthesized brass section, keyboards and bass added to the drums. The rock (1-*2*-3-*4*) rhythm is complemented by the bass filling in (*1*-2-*3*-4), together achieving a steady 1-2-3-4 at a quick tempo that excites you. Mariah Carey starts singing lyrics that burst with excitement about the depth and height she now experiences with her emotions, since meeting someone special.

She asserts her love and renewed vitality, describing feelings of ecstacy and the wondrous response to a lover's tender touch. Carey is able to emphasize her words with different voice inflections and pitches. For instance, her voice jumps past thirteen notes to land on a very high G for "inside." Then, she does it again, hitting the high G in the next verse. In fact, she likes it so much she plays around in that range, more than once, and then laughingly ends the song on a low note. "Emotions" definitely emphasizes one category of feeling: enthusiastic excitement.

For similar mood-matching enthusiasm, try "Hallelujah" from the Clark Sister's *Black Gospel Explosion*, BeauSoleil's "Jeunes

Filles de Quatorze Ans" (zydeco), 2 Unlimited's "Let the Beat Control Your Body" (techno rock), or the following selection, "Swept Away."

MUSIC SELECTION:	"Swept Away" (8:30) from *Live at the Acropolis* (new age/jazz)
COMPOSER/ARTIST:	Yanni
INSTRUMENTATION:	Keyboards, violin, bass, drums, percussion, full orchestra

Commentary: This Acropolis concert culminated Yanni's dream of performing in his native country. "Swept Away" is one of the concert's high-energy pieces that celebrates his homecoming to Greece.

The drums start out very fast with many notes, holding a straight 1-2 beat. That combination brings your mood immediately to what I call a "robust" feeling. The melodic line is tossed back and forth between keyboards and violin as the original rhythm continues. Then a samba rhythm is introduced by the piano, with the brass responding. The guitar plays a rhythmic solo, which is taken over by the percussion, then tossed to the keyboards. The violin turns it into a lively jazz improv. The orchestra grabs it and the brass win. Underneath, the drums' rhythmic pattern never stops. The keyboards take back the original melody as the orchestra returns to the Brazilian rhythms that end "Swept Away." All this inner activity drives the music to a high-energy peak, enhanced by the special electricity of a live performance.

Other music that may match this mood of enthusiasm includes Michael Gettel's "Fire from the Sky" from *The Art of Nature* (new age), Mark O'Connor's "Orange Blossom Special" (country), Herbie Hancock's "Dis Is Da Drum" (jazz), and the next selection, "Presto."

MUSIC SELECTION:	"Presto" (8:15) from "Symphony No. 7 in A Major" (classical)
COMPOSER:	Ludwig Von Beethoven (1770–1827)
INSTRUMENTATION:	Full orchestra

Commentary: As the orchestra moves through the music, the rhythmic phrases are always being tossed to other instruments, and pitches and timbres are switching, all of which keeps the music lively and interesting. Interludes of woodwinds play a slower melody, which is answered by the strings in call-responses. This creates calm, lulling moments in the music. After each lull, the original enthusiastic melody returns to pick up your energy. This music is a great cure for classical music phobia.

If you like the enthusiasm evoked by "Presto," also try "Presto" from Mozart's "Symphony No. 35," "Hallelujah Chorus" from Handel's the "Messiah" (both classical), "Just One World" from Craig Chaquico's *Acoustic Planet* (new age/new country), or Nicholas Gunn's "Odessa" from *The Sacred Fire* (new age).

In reading this section's four chapters, matching particular moods to specific music, have you noticed any music that may belong in a gray area, between Unsettling and Soothing or Soothing and Energizing? If so, you might consider USEing these music works to help you make easier transitions from very Unsettling to ultra Soothing to extremely Energizing music. Sometimes the shock of strong music may be as disconcerting as waking up to an alarm clock. When lighter music is USEd to bridge categories, you have an opportunity to adapt to the emotional message of the music elements. Examples of this will be included in my assessments in the next chapter, which contains true stories from people across the country who have included music in their daily lives, for better or for worse.

Music

at Work:

HEALING PRINCIPLES IN PRACTICE

11

True Stories:

What Helps,
What Hinders

IN MY WORK as a music therapist, and specifically for this book, I have asked many people to share with me their feelings about music, whether positive or negative. They talk about how music has affected them, and I talk about how they USEd it—or could have USEd it. To respect their privacy, identification details have been changed, but the essential heart of their stories and their interactions with music remains.

What makes any one individual like any particular kind of music? The elements within music itself, reviewed in the second chapter, are one part of the equation; the second part consists of the elements within your own life: your cultural/familial roots, age, work environment, and health.

Your family background, cultural heritage, and the era in which you grew up—these are your roots, and influence you a great deal, both in what you turn to and what you try to leave behind. Moreover, you associate certain values, consciously or not, with the good times you experienced in any one era and, by association, its music. The age factor ties in with that, since "age" here is defined more by accumulated life experiences rather than by number of years. Work environment is considered because, with the national economic concern with productivity, more and more studies are being done concerning what factors influence people to work more effectively. I'm a true believer in taking your music to work. The component of health weights your response to music because poor health often makes it difficult for you to focus on anything else. The good news is that when you USE the music system you have learned, you can improve your health.

In my experience, two other more ephemeral—at least, less quantifiable—elements come into play regarding music preferences. "Music and memories" recur time after time as a theme when people are asked about music. It is obvious that this aspect of music has tremendous inherent power. Part of therapeutic music intervention is honoring the meaningfulness of that particular piece of music for the individual, then to help him or her find new ways, and new music, to validate equally positive feelings.

A second sticking point with music is that people decide they like one style, perhaps two, and have little motivation or curiosity to look beyond their preferences. It is wonderful to find people who treasure any music, but when their choices go from firm to rigid it becomes counterproductive. Don't limit yourself; be open to integrating new music into your life. Again, the point is to find more ways to experience positive moments and new resources for healing when the negative times come.

As you read through the following brief accounts, consider what is relevant to your own life, confrontations, and joyful moments. My commentaries are directed to the individuals involved in the accounts, but I invite you to extract what applies to you and to find the pertinent healing message.

Music and Memories

For some people, hearing a particular song or music work brings an instant smile: good memories are evoked. For others, music harshly recalls traumatic memories; even the most calming music can have discordant associations. One woman told me she "hates lullabies"; it took a while to find out that her mother had never sung them to her, never showed any maternal warmth. Music can both recover "peaceful, easy feelings" and open up old wounds. Thus emotional associations play a major role, not in the ability of music to heal, but in your ability to allow music to heal you.

The following accounts illustrate varying situations in which music helped bring about healing.

When I was a teenager. . .
"When I'd go through the most devastating events—at least they seemed that way—listening to a slow piece of music helped me then: Joni Mitchell's 'Blue.' To this day I still find myself going back to it. I remember listening to the Grateful Dead and think-ing how in synch they are with their audience. 'Dark Star' was an incredible bonding song for me and my friends. We'd look at each other and know we all were feeling the same thing. It was as if the Dead knew exactly what we were experiencing."
—ROD MORGENSTEIN, DRUMMER FOR THE DIXIE DREGS

INTERPRETATION: Mood matching at its optimum. Painful emotions were eased by listening to Joni Mitchell's album "Blue" and still can be, if the listener gives the music that power. It is possible that if music on this album were followed by music from the Soothing to Energizing categories, the working through process could be com-pleted faster. "Dark Star's" music elements may provoke Unsettled feelings of melancholy for listeners who lack the positive connec-tion with the Grateful Dead. For fans, the Grateful Dead embarks on an emotional journey that makes them feel great.

"My parents were always yelling about the stuff I'd done, more often their list of what I hadn't done. I'd slam the door of my room and drown it in Pink Floyd, Led Zeppelin, and Bruce Springsteen. I actually got sort of annoyed when my mother started liking Springsteen. I've gone to a couple of the new tour concerts. We're older now with jobs and families, but the emo-tional experience is still intense."
—JACK, ENVIRONMENTALIST, EARLY THIRTIES

INTERPRETATION: This is a typical reaction of a younger generation jealously guarding "my music"—especially when the music is used to accentuate generational differences, as in Jack's story. I recall one woman who was outraged that teenagers are listening to and liking Gregorian chant, specifically, the unexpected hit *Chant* by Spanish Benedictine monks. She considered it "so out-of-character" for them, because her father had liked to listen to it! To her, it was the music that "belonged" to her father; teenagers were trespassers. An older woman reminded her that we all have emotions that need to be expressed, and that she should be glad teens are being touched by this music.

For Jack, his emotional experience continues to be intense because of his strong memory associations. He doesn't need to negate that, but I'd like to see him look for other styles of music that relate to who he is now, in addition to what reminds him of the past.

Because of my mother. . .
"My parents divorced when I was five, and my dad split after two years, to Hawaii. I found myself at that cartoon age [seven to ten years old] really liking my Mom's silly music, now called "novelty" songs: 'Purple People Eater,' 'Beep Beep,' 'Monster Mash,' 'Short Shorts.' They're like cartoons for my ears and I always get a dumb smile on my face when I hear them on some oldies station."
—FRED V., MID-TWENTIES

INTERPRETATION: It's amazing how children automatically choose music that will help them feel better. Fred's parents' divorce was a harsh reality for him, and these songs brought him cheerful relief. For Fred, that music will always bring a smile to his face—memory associations once again. Other music selections he might use to achieve this same state without nostalgia come from the Energizing category. Young children in similar situations might also like "Zip-A-Dee-Doo-Da," "Hakuna Matata" from "The Lion King" or "Aladdin's" "A Whole New World." Therapy techniques that combine creative arts therapies (music, art, dance/movement, drama/psychodrama, poetry) are particularly effective in cutting through and balancing children's troubled emotions.

When I remember what helped in the bad times. . .
"I was told to practice breathing techniques after I suffered a collapsed lung at age thirty-five, so I joined a singing class. We all had

to bring in a favorite song to sing. There were many different people and we all brought in different kinds of songs. I brought in the Eagles' 'Desperado,' because, when I first heard it, I was also going through bad times, and I knew it would help me to sing it now."

—ANN, POLICE INVESTIGATOR, LATE-THIRTIES

INTERPRETATION: Ann is reaching out to music that helped her get through personal troubles years ago. It helps her now at another level—she's singing to it. When you connect a song to your mood, singing it through has much more impact than simply listening to it. You're actually saying the words that describe your state of mind, to music that makes you feel the words dramatically. Just as Mr. Shahrooz and Natalie Cole described their emotional experiences while performing blues music (chapter 4), singing or playing the music can be a cathartic experience. If you can't play an instrument, sing—off-key, on-key, who cares? This is just for you.

When I met my wife. . .
"We were in junior high in a string quartet, playing Schubert's 'Rosamunde Overture,' she on viola, me on violin. Every time we hear that overture now, we both remember. . .well, a lot of good things."

—JAMES, RETIRED ADMINISTRATOR, MID-SIXTIES

INTERPRETATION: Two things are at work here. First, the experience of playing music together provides a bridge that builds lasting relationships. A recent research study brought teenagers together with senior citizens to sing in a community choir, and the attitudes of the generations toward one another were significantly improved as a result.[1] Second, in James' case, memory association is at work whenever he and his wife hear the "Rosamunde Overture," which stimulates positive feelings.

When I danced with my husband. . .
"During one bad night, of the several bad nights caused by a severely pulled muscle in my back, I still couldn't sleep. So I played Strauss waltzes and began to imagine waltzing with my husband, who had died years ago. I became less aware of the pain as I danced alone. This brought back the wonderful memories of dancing with

him in our big family room. Our children would get embarrassed,
and run to pull down the blinds so the neighbors couldn't see.
Because I was so totally relaxed at the end of the music, all the pain
was gone, so I went to bed and slept like a baby."
                    —TERESA, FITNESS WALKING GUIDE, EARLY SEVENTIES

INTERPRETATION: It is impossible to feel two emotions simultaneously.[2] Consequently, when music creates emotions that oppose
the emotions created by pain, the pain can be alleviated. This was
what Teresa experienced. Her emotions of love and joy (coupled
with the therapy of dancing) drove away the emotions of anxiety
and tension, and she experienced a cessation of pain.

Because my husband asked. . .
"The day before my husband's death (at age sixty-nine) he knew
he wasn't going to make it, so we planned his funeral. He told me
that he wanted to have only light and happy country music played
at the funeral, like Patsy Cline's 'Life's Railway to Heaven' and
Marty Robbins' 'El Paso,' and we spent some very close moments
carefully planning the music together. People told me afterward
how warm and delightful the service was, which made me feel
better, and it did seem true to my husband's spirit."
                    —LUCILLE J., COMMUNITY VOLUNTEER, EARLY SIXTIES

INTERPRETATION: Preprogramming music may be important at a
party but it is crucial in matters of the heart. Lucille's husband did
not want a lugubrious ceremony. He wanted the guests who came
to his funeral to experience the feelings that, hopefully, he himself
had brought to their lives.

A recent memorial service I attended for a fellow musician had
similar results. Even though he knew of his impending death, his
response to his wife's query about the funeral was, "Play
Mozart's clarinet concerto and maybe some guys will get up and
play." After he died, she programmed music for the memorial service that helped people achieve an emotional catharsis, ending
with positive feelings rather than mournfulness.

People heard Mozart's clarinet concerto while filtering in.
Then, a trombone choir comprised of her husband's colleagues
played music that began somberly and ended with heroic brass

harmonies. Featured during the service was a joyful recording of the deceased playing his "signature" trombone solo, variations on "The Blue Bells of Scotland." No one else could play it quite the same. In spite of the man's tragic death from cancer, his friends and family were left with the message of hope that was so important to him.

I'm not about to advise anyone on the most appropriate ambiance of a memorial for a loved one, but perhaps it would help to know that not only dirges and sad hymns are possible. If you are interested in this idea, other uplifting music to consider might be "Achieved His Glorious Work" by Haydn (classical), Enya's new age "Orinoco Flow," selections from the Christian recordings *Instruments of Praise* by the Tom Keene Orchestra, and Steven and Annie Chapman's "Does Jesus Care" from *Times and Seasons.*

Because of my daughter...
"Back in the '50s my daughter contracted polio when we were stationed in Korea. She spent three months in a hospital in physical therapy. On the day my wife and I came to pick her up we couldn't find her in her room. The office told us that because it was after three o'clock, she would be out in the back garden entertaining the troops. We were puzzled and went to look for her. We found her with about forty severely wounded Korean soldiers, some with missing body parts, some with crushed heads, some blind, some with crushed faces and, in general, the most severely wounded men I had ever seen. And most of them were crying.

"Barbara was two years old and paralyzed from the waist down. We saw her leaning on her crutches and singing her heart out in a Korean lullaby: Tokki-san, nabi-san... (Little rabbit, little chipmunk...). The nurse told us that Barbara's singing had a definite calming effect on this aggressive, very difficult group of men, who felt their government had failed them."
—MICHAEL, RETIRED ARMY OFFICER, AGE SIXTY-SIX

INTERPRETATION: Little children are open books of feelings. The young girl only saw that the soldiers were hurt and she wanted to help them, not thinking about herself. Her instincts about music's healing power were right. For her father, this reflection is not about music in general but about a crystallized moment in time, first, when he saw the effect of a child's openhearted love and, second, the effect of a lullaby on grown men. This has become symbolic to him of what music's power means.

Because of my mother. . .
"I like the old-style country music, because my mom listened to it. Dad died from cancer when I was four and mom never remarried. She took care of us seven kids by cleaning houses and baby-sitting. I chose Jim Reeves' 'In the Garden' for mom's funeral. I listen to this song now when I'm down and just let the tape finish. It brings back sad memories of her death, but good memories of how much she loved us."
                                    —BETTY, HOMEMAKER, MID-SIXTIES

INTERPRETATION: See the commentary after the next story.

"I could never understand why, in my younger days, when all of my friends were rockin' out to the Beatles, I would often cut out and listen to Andy Williams and Nat King Cole. I mentioned this a while back to my mother and she got all emotional. She told me that was the music she always played when she would rock me to sleep. Ever since I found that out, I've rocked my two-year-old son to sleep with Andy Williams and Nat King Cole."
                                    —HIROSHI, CONTRACTOR, MID-FORTIES

INTERPRETATION: Music can tie generations together through troubled times. When Betty's forty-something son heard his grandmother's favorite "In the Garden" sung recently during a church Easter service, he was overwhelmed with tears. That started his young son crying; both had been at the funeral and loved grandma/great-grandma. When Hiroshi's son is grown I wonder if Andy Williams and Nat King Cole will be his favorites? The recordings of these two singers' mellifluous voices are complemented by lush string arrangements. The combined effect produces Soothing emotions of tenderness and love, which you might also find in classical selections like "Fantasia on Greensleeves" and Debussy's "Clair de Lune," or the popular hit "Evergreen" from the film "A Star is Born."

Because of my dad. . .
"To make extra money during the war (World War II), my dad, who was in the RAF, played the double bass in bands the RAF would loan to the Americans. After the war, he became a research technician but he still kept playing, just for fun, and I grew up listening to the big band sounds and a lot of improvisational jazz on the radio and with my dad's friends. He was such a great father, such a support, that when I hear that music, I always feel good."
—DENISE, OFFICE ADMINISTRATOR, MID-FORTIES

INTERPRETATION: Music memories can remind us of positive relationships we had with our parents. That music then comes to represent our reverence for them, evoking in us feelings of love and pride. Those feelings, in turn, enhance self-esteem and increase our ability to interact positively with others.

After the divorce. . .
"After the divorce I deliberately put music out of my life. Too many pieces raised too many memories. All music meant loss and longing."
—JANET, DIVORCED MOTHER OF TWO, EARLY FORTIES

INTERPRETATION: Janet connected music only with "loss and longing." She denied and repressed her feelings, and didn't USE music that could have helped her, and in so doing, probably stayed Unsettled longer than necessary. If you let it, music can offer a gentle, nonthreatening way to deal with emotional challenges. With sequenced listening to appropriate music, Janet might have been able to move more easily through her feelings of loss and onward to Soothed and Energized emotions.

Because of my parents. . .
"I grew up with music, because my mother was a pianist and my father a singer. They were so caught up in their careers. They played joyful music, but there was no joy in my family. My mother would lock me out of the house so that I couldn't disturb her practicing. My whole life became about not *feeling. Learning to heal myself years later was hard. If I did hear happy music, I knew that it was full of all the things I wouldn't allow myself to*

feel, and tears would come. That would feed my fear of letting my emotions come out."
                    —CARLA, HOLISTIC HEALTH PRACTITIONER, MID-FIFTIES

INTERPRETATION: For Carla, any loving connection with her parents was denied because their own feelings of love and joy were restricted to musical expression, with nothing left over for her. Years later, working hard to find an escape from her own resultant emotional deadlock, she USEd a special music tape that she soon nicknamed her "personal therapist." The tape sequenced music matching specific emotions, including Wagner's "Ride of the Valkyries" for agitation, "Fogflute" from Thompson's *Isle of Skye* for stillness, and Chabrier's "Espana" for optimism.

"Only Christian music was allowed in our house, so I had to go to my friends' houses to listen to Pearl Jam and Stone Temple Pilots. I finally got my own place, and now I put my feet up on the table, turn the bass up, and listen to alternative for hours. It's the most totally relaxing thing I know."
                                    —MIKE, ENGINEER, MID-TWENTIES

INTERPRETATION: Walls of parent/child misunderstanding could be torn down by a sincere attempt to understand children's choices. A healthful way of approaching Mike's favorite music would be to understand what feelings those two music groups provoked in him and why he had those feelings to begin with. Restricting his access to something that helped him vent an Unsettled mood actually kept the mood Unsettled. Since Mike then rebelled or withdrew, the frustration and anger on both sides increased.

Ask your children how the music makes them feel, even if they consider you weird for asking. Somewhere inside, they notice that you cared enough to ask. This is difficult for parents to do with any kind of flair, since adolescents frequently consider them hopelessly backward about music. Ask anyway, but keep it light. No inquisition, just an "I care about you" opportunity.

At this point, could Mike help himself further? Yes. Mike is relaxing due to the feeling of freedom as much as to the music, since that's his emotional connection with alternative rock. I'd like to see him give himself more options. When rock music has slow tempos, harmonious melodies, and rhythm filled in with even accents, relaxation may occur more easily than with rock that features fast tempo, dissonance, and a heavy 1-2-3-4 rhythm. Besides the conditioned relaxing effect alternative rock had on Mike, he could first explore other rock substyles from Soothing and Energizing, such as trance and techno rock, to get accustomed to stimulating different moods, then begin crossing over to other styles like jazz, world, and classical. He could do this at his own pace, as he became accustomed to the new music.

I had to take music lessons. . .
"I had to take piano lessons until fifth grade, but I was only interested in sports. One day at my lesson, when it was obvious I had substituted playing softball for practicing one time too many, my teacher marched me out to my mother who was waiting in the car. She said I didn't have a musical bone in my body and she was giving up."

—STEVEN, WHO WENT ON TO BECOME A
THREE-SPORT LETTERMAN IN HIGH SCHOOL AND
A MEMBER OF THE GLENN MILLER BAND

INTERPRETATION: Fortunately, Steven was later guided by a high school music teacher who could see his talent and develop it. Too many music teachers teach "by the book," rather than by adapting their techniques to meet the students' needs. I know, however, of one pragmatic piano teacher who requires students who are interested in basketball to dribble a ball daily for fifteen minutes, in addition to their regular piano practice. She informs them that both piano playing and basketball require strength and flexibility in wrist muscles. It certainly hooks the students. Do I think all music teachers with reluctant students will do this? No, but I do think it helps to be open to new techniques in any field.

The song stayed in my head. . .
"During a really lonely period, I was falling asleep to the radio and heard a Mozart violin concerto. It was the loneliest sound I'd ever heard, but it was gorgeous. I didn't hear what the name of the music was, so I bought all the concertos, then all the sonatas, but I have never heard that same sound again. Maybe because I'm not in the same place emotionally anymore."

—KAREN, ARTIST, LATE TWENTIES

INTERPRETATION: See commentary after next story.

"I always wondered if anyone else had the same experience I did: I'd be walking along, or working at something, and find myself humming, but I wouldn't remember what the song was. Hours, maybe days later, I'd remember the title and then realize that the lyrics to that particular song totally matched whatever problem or happy feeling was important to me at that time."
—LIZ, EXECUTIVE RECRUITER, EARLY THIRTIES

INTERPRETATION: Karen and Liz discovered how music can act as a chameleon. For Karen, the same music selection, played by the same group, had a totally different effect on her because she was in a different emotional place when she heard it again. The fact that she still looks for music to match that mood tells me that she is still experiencing similar feelings. However, it's difficult to recommend specific music for therapy unless I know what she felt about her life condition at that time and how those emotions and conditions are similar, yet different, today.

Liz's account is interesting because she claims she hardly ever listens to music, yet music and lyrics underscored a basic truth in her life more than once. She considers that slightly odd, but it would be good for her to talk through which songs remind her of particular problems or good feelings. She could work from that point to find any number of music possibilities that could bring about important, positive changes in her life.

The memory context of music can affect performers as well, as they deal with audience responses. Singer Natalie Cole offered a personal anecdote:

"It took many years before I could feel comfortable performing my father's songs, because I found that the effect my father's music had on the audience when I sang it was much different from the effect he had had. When I sang it people would start crying. That upset me very, very much. They started crying because of the emotional connection, because my father was no longer living, and here I was in my twenties, doing his music. It brought back a flood of memories for them, and was really overwhelming for a lot of people. And that scared me, so I backed off and only did R & B and pop."
—NATALIE COLE, SINGER AND DAUGHTER OF NAT KING COLE

INTERPRETATION: Even though while in her twenties Natalie's experience of singing her father's music was a negative one, it actually was positive for her audiences. Watching her sing her father's songs took them on an emotional journey that resulted in a cathartic release, an experience that moved them from grief (for him and perhaps a bit for their own bygone youth) to love to joy at seeing his daughter following in his footsteps. Natalie herself came to terms with her own love for her father's music—so tied to her love and to respect for the man himself—and the emotional effect that music evoked in her audiences. The emotionality now becomes a shared experience, a bonding of performer and audience.

Holding on to this positive aspect of music and memories, I would now like to look closer at age, work environment, health, and the composite panorama of "roots"—part the era of your youth, part cultural heritage. Music speaks to us about ourselves in many ways: we resonate with the sound of our own lives' passages.

The significance of heritage is a spectrum in itself, from nonexistent to mildly interesting to tremendously important, and attitudes about music reflect this. For example, within America's cultural mosaic, many people dislike "ethnic music," especially their own. Yet, in later years, it becomes a grounding influence. In it they find a sense of going home. Rap has meaning for listeners who see it as representing the real world, their culture, and, in some cases, threats to their culture. A consistent topic in music therapy workshops is the effectiveness of music that evokes heritage awareness. The next story reflects the wider, often unarticulated emotional response shared by many.

Nana J. gets in touch with her roots when she goes on long drives. Singing karaoke-style, Nana plays her Native American tapes and sings in her Navajo tongue. "My father is a medicine man, and from him I've developed a deep appreciation for our sacred and secular music. I love to hear or sing the songs that the Navajo have created for every occasion, whether it's for everyday living, rocking a baby, corn grinding or horse riding. And even though I live many miles away from there, this music connects me to my parents and the reservation I miss so much."

INTERPRETATION: Living away from a culture you value can be stressful and can create hardships. Listening to the music of your heritage can reaffirm your connection to that culture and renew your personal commitment and goals, especially if circumstances prevent you from going back to places that are important in your life. Even people who think they are much too sophisticated to care often find themselves moved or cheered by the music of their roots. Nana cared very much and knew it. She used the music of her heritage at a time when she was alone for an extended period of time—long drives. Instead of being a chore, the long drives became opportunities for Nana to center herself.

Age

We tend to think of certain age groups favoring certain music. Largely, that holds true, but I think it's less a function of absolute age than your perception of what your life has been about. When was the "prime of your life"? When did you feel most secure, with your whole life still ahead of you? During what period were you absorbed in defining yourself as a person? The music that was current during that time is probably going to remain the music you most love and relate to. For instance, in 2025, today's teenagers will still get good feelings from the music of Boyz II Men, Aerosmith, Metallica, and Digital Underground. Although the following stories focus on the individual's age, other dynamics also come into play.

Louis H. aspires to join the NFL. At age fifteen, six feet tall and 210 pounds, he received the Best Defensive Player Award for his high school football team. Since the third grade he's loved rap, and has accumulated a collection of fifty-plus rap CDs. "I rev up before a game to 'Section 8' Mob and 'Volume 10.' Rappin' along with the music gives me a rush, gets me going." Louis considers himself a rap puritan and says, "Most rappers are frustrated. You can tell the difference in rappers by the way they feel. I don't really care about what the words say. It's the feeling behind it. A good rapper talks about bad things goin' on—because that's the reality of the world."

INTERPRETATION: Rap has been a positive experience for Louis; the downside is that it's practically the only music he listens to. Frustrations can be perpetuated when other music, which would bring out a healthy range of emotions, is denied. Louis' first step might be to think about music styles that incorporate some of what he likes about rap, to strengthen his music collection. The beat so predominant in rap music can be found in hip-hop, world (African), jazz, and rock. Lyrical similarity could be found in alternative rock, for example, in the group Counting Crows. Listening to these new sources may provide an easier transition to other styles and emotions that are optimally Soothing and/or Energizing, eventually opening up classical music for Louis as well.

Mike H., a part-time football official and full-time vice president of a title insurance company, is an avid Rush Limbaugh listener because, "Rush replaces newspapers and tells the truth." Mike's son is Louis, and his frustrations with the world, at age forty-something, are similar to his son's. Their anger is expressed in the kind of music they both like. In his "early" angry years, the Rolling Stones was Mike's favorite group. The Stone's music has now been augmented with the alternative rock of Counting Crows—different dark feelings. But Mike also listens to country at a bar and jazz in the car—Michael Franks' "Dragonfly Summer" and Incognito's "Positivity."

INTERPRETATION: Mike is already crossing over into other music styles, which may lead him to explore classical, easy listening, new age, gospel, and Christian, to evoke more Soothing moods and different degrees of Energizing ones. He can continue to influence Louis' emotional balance during family times, for example, playing Soothing music during meal times. His son may groan, but it will offer a calm interlude, a time to share good food and the day's events. Even if nobody talks, the music playing in the background will have a subtle, calming effect.

Megan R. is a professional dancer and, at age twenty-three, part of the demographic 'Generation X.' To energize before going on stage to dance Tchaikovsky's ballet 'The Nutcracker,' Megan listens with headphones to a special tape she made of U2, Erasure, 'James Brown Is Dead' by techno group L.A. Style, and other rock music.

INTERPRETATION: Megan's instincts are right on. USEing music not only as an energizer but as a distraction is correct. Even though it seems dichotomous—a dancer involved with classical music listening to techno rock—Megan is USEing music just as many musicians do: listening to something they like but which is completely different from what must be performed, so that the performance is fresh and focused. Later, Megan might find a "cool down" benefit after the performance by matching her Energizing mood first with techno rock or classical music, followed by trance, classical, or new age music in the Soothing realm.

Tony S., a fourteen-year-old musician and straight A student, listens to classical music to fall asleep, wake up, and study. "The slow music of piano sonatinas relaxes me and the big boisterous music of Aaron Copland, Mozart, and the 'William Tell Overture' gets me going. What makes me happy? Aerosmith and the Doors."

Tony's best friend since age two is Dennis W., a first-string football player who prefers heavy metal and alternative music for almost any mood—Metallica, Green Day, Offspring, and Nirvana. "When I'm alone listening to Metallica I feel like I'm in the middle of their concert with lots of people. When I'm mad, their slower stuff calms me down. When going to sleep, I just turn the volume down. I know Metallica's 'Fade to Black' helped me relax when I was playing football."

INTERPRETATION: Tony and Dennis continue to be good friends; conflicting music preferences just aren't important to them. Both are accessing similar emotions of relaxation and happiness in very different music, and future conversations between them could explore that. Meanwhile, despite all the debate about the impact of lyrics on the mind, Dennis was adamant about heavy metal lyrics *not* motivating killer desires. Could it be possible that these lyrics and the matching music could be correctly USEd to *release* pent-up emotions, instead of acting as a catalyst to activate them? It's worth considering.

Work Environment

Do you have to listen to piped-in music that's not your style, or does your office mate move to a different rhythm of life and music? If so, that could move you to learn to appreciate new music styles—or move you to request a transfer!

As an education administrator, Frank P. kept music playing in his office because it helped him concentrate. When he retired, he and his wife Carol moved further into the Alaskan bush, taking their entire music collection with them. Their stereo system, and all other electrical appliances are powered by a diesel generator that charges a row of golf cart batteries. Frank has a portable CD player in his workshop. For work that requires concentration and fine hand movement, he recommends Vivaldi's "The Four Seasons" and Mozart symphonies. (As this book was going to press, his first project—a Kitfox airplane—was licensed.)

INTERPRETATION: Numerous studies cite classical music as being particularly helpful for concentration, although I would not recommend it from the Unsettling category if relaxed concentration is necessary. The music of Vivaldi and Mozart has regular rhythms, varied tempos to keep your interest, and pleasing melodies and timbres. Other good classical choices would be the relaxing music of "Adagio" from Saint-Saens' "Organ Symphony in C# minor," Pachelbel's "Canon in D major," and the "Minuet" from Gluck's "Orpheus and Eurydice."

Joe D., a thirty-two-year-old computer analyst, had a music library overflowing with classical music and little else. At work, in a shared office space, he was deluged with rock 'n' roll. Little wonder that his ulcerative colitis continued to get worse until he literally rearranged his life. "In one year I changed jobs, girlfriends, and finished college. My new coworker is more amenable to classical music, and I'm learning to like rock more. I don't even mind the commute that goes with this job because I put together a special driving tape, combining Nirvana with Puccini!"

INTERPRETATION: For a stressful situation, Joe, who truly prefers classical music but is opening up to rock, might begin with Unsettling music such as Mahler's "Symphony No. 2," Prokofiev's "Symphony No. 5," or Pearl Jam's grunge style. For Soothing choices I would recommend he consider not only Bach chamber music and Beethoven piano sonatas, but also Vivaldi, Mozart, and Soothing film soundtrack medleys.

In the office, the use of music by one person may inspire another to create his or her own music environment, with preferred radio stations or tapes and CDs. Then cacophony can result, as volumes increase to drown out neighboring music. There's little you can do if your music annoys others or vice versa. Courtesy and good business sense indicate putting on the headphones. For work situations where that is not possible or not allowed, I'd recommend that you initiate discussion with coworkers and the appropriate manager. Another avenue is to get a consensus of music style preferences in each work area and set up a schedule of specific CDs/tapes or radio stations (e.g., Muzak provides all sixteen music styles herein, plus individual ethnic or national styles—Latino, French, Irish, etc.).

Joe's driving tape is an excellent example of how to handle stress in the car. Since getting to work is often hard work in itself, it's relevant to sidestep briefly to consider the stress of commuting and the observations of Roger L., age thirty-five, who drives a truck for a living.

"When I listen to hard rock I get very aggressive and short-tempered, cutting people off in traffic. With soft rock or country music, I am much more patient, and I let 'em pass."

INTERPRETATION: Roger has found the key to controlling his anger, the most common emotion found among drivers. Music elements in hard rock, particularly rhythm, timbre, and melody, are more forceful and demanding while these same elements in soft rock effectively sound more mellow. For combating fatigue and boredom on long-distance drives, you'll find many selections in the Energizing groups, similar to the works of Nirvana and Puccini, found on Joe's driving tape.

The concept of music in the workplace was succinctly explained by Jean N., a business management consultant with several clients in the factory settings and manufacturing industries.

"Employees have many challenges, often sitting for long hours performing repetitive tasks. I have seen remarkable improvements in morale and production by adding music to the environment. I am very determined to get the results I desire, and will continue to

change the music until I get the desired results: to raise the profit margin for the company and to benefit the employees."

Some people have told Jean that she uses music to manipulate situations.

She responds, "True, but in my own defense, I am using music, aroma therapy, and a positive attitude to get what the employees need. After all, people set different moods all the time without realizing the power of their efforts. What do we see or read about a romantic scene? The lights are dimmed, beautiful, soft music is playing, flowers add fragrance and color—this is manipulation at its finest!!"

INTERPRETATION: "Manipulation" is a word with a negative connotation. The concept of a therapeutic aid to make work life easier and more effective is the true meaning here. There are far too many work sites where music is not permitted at all, and the factories and offices of corporate America could benefit from some musical restructuring.

Let's now consider the component in your ability to respond to music to which you may give little importance—until, as the truism goes, you lose it: your health.

General Health

In addition to the range of emotions you experience on any given day, you may be allergic to whatever is blowing in the wind this season. A broken limb may constrict you, or a sprained ankle may test your endurance. Working and living on overtime may jeopardize your regular sleep routine. Functional handicaps physically challenge some and demoralize others. Arthritis can become debilitating and frustrating, and a life-threatening illness can drive every other thought from your mind. Even with generally good physical health, emotional and mental stress seem to be endemic to living in the twentieth century.

It is true that "stress," which automatically has negative connotations for most people, does, in fact, have a good side as well. Stress encountered and used well has been the focus of numerous studies citing that CEOs outlive others. "They're in control and rise above 'negative stress.' Instead, they experience 'positive stress,' which helps them focus on work—and play."[3] Unfortunately, most people do not handle stress this way and fall into the opposite category: the stress experienced by many Americans cost industry $10 to $20 billion annually through lost work days, hospitalization, and early death.[4]

Because the effects of negative stress are well-documented, I will discuss it in that context. Your ability to connect with a wide range of music, at specific times, may alleviate your stress. For Person A, some low, slow Soothing sounds may be the only music that helps. Person B may need authoritative, energetic music. For Person C, depression may turn to irritation rather than happiness, if only energetic music is heard. You will find music that best suits you, but the optimum choice may be different for each stressful situation. Meanwhile, the following stories, which explain how music reduced stress and pain for some people, may help you build your own music antistress defenses.

In my work at counseling centers, I offered preprogrammed music for the centers' clients, as an option while waiting for their counseling sessions. One man decided to listen to an eleven-minute special tape before seeing his therapist. Afterward, he cornered me and proceeded to criticize the music, what was wrong with it, and what he would have preferred. When I asked if he had noticed any difference within himself after listening to the music, he stopped talking, thought a minute, and exclaimed, "I've had this aching chest pain since I came here a week ago, and now it's gone!"

INTERPRETATION: Even though the music was not exactly what this man would have selected, it still worked, because this eleven-minute specialized tape sequenced music selections that matched Unsettled to Soothed to Energized moods. This was based on the premise that most people waiting for a counseling session would indeed be in one or more Unsettled conditions—anger, distress, fear, sorrow, etc. With the sequencing, they would have an opportunity to work through the bad stuff, give themselves Soothing respite, and reEnergize themselves at the end. Two of the pieces on that particular tape were "Pruit Igoe" from the soundtrack of the film "Koyaanisqatsi" and new ager Ray Lynch's "Celestial Soda Pop." (Both are found in chapter 7.)

The man's reaction also suggested a possible correlation between his chest pain and an emotional imbalance, which I hope he discussed with his counselor.

(**Note:** This particular situation highlights music therapy as an adjunct to another therapeutic resource. It is important to know that music therapists interact with other therapy practitioners and are also skilled in combined interventions of music therapy and counseling.)

> ". . .Clinical experience and many anecdotal and sporadic studies all confirm the benefits of music therapy in preventing potentially fatal conditions, enhancing patients' well-being, shortening their hospital stay, and increasing their independence thereafter. . ."
>
> —Matthew H. M. Lee, M.D., MPH
> "Forever Young: Music and Aging"
> U.S. Senate Special Committee on Aging Conference
> August 1, 1991

"Just before sinus surgery, I listened to Peter Gabriel's 'Us' and 'So,' and 'Watermark' by Enya. That music completely exhilarated me, and I put the headphones back on during recovery. That experience made me realize that I would have fared much better during my vasectomy last year if I had used similar music. With the used and abused feeling during that surgery preparation, I felt intensely degraded. Then, because only a local [anesthetic] was used, I felt a shooting pain clear into my chest—twice! I know now that that music would have helped. I came close to crying after both surgeries—the vasectomy because I felt so bad, and the sinus operation because I felt so good."
—ALLEN P., MARKETING EXECUTIVE, LATE THIRTIES

INTERPRETATION: Interestingly, Peter Gabriel's CD "So" includes "Mercy Street," listed in the Unsettling chapter as music that evokes depression. In Allen's case, he absolutely loves Peter Gabriel and has many wonderful memory associations with all of Gabriel's music, thus, his responsive exhilaration. It is also possible that the pain during the other surgical procedure could have been reduced. For instance, many music therapists use the GIM (Guided Imagery & Music) technique, combining music and specific mental images. This is a drug-free music therapy application that utilizes visualization processes with music specially chosen for the individual.

"[Dr. Chase's regular performances at Beverly Manor Convalescent Hospital result in] residents with severe depression and residents with Alzheimer's suddenly perk up and their eyes sparkle and hands and feet tap to the tunes. . .music is a visible healer every Thursday afternoon."

—KERRY D. DAVIS, ADMINISTRATOR[5]
(TAKEN FROM SENATE REPORT PREVIOUSLY REFERENCED)

INTERPRETATION: I applaud this doctor's openness to utilizing music for health. He visited these patients not as a physician but as a giver of care via music; as a physician he had an additional capability for evaluating the effect his music was having. His skill as a violinist was an extension of the personal appreciation of music many M.D.s share, and when physicians discover personal experiences with music's healing benefit, they are much more apt to be advocates for music therapy intervention. Hospitals are becoming much more aware of music's possibilities, as this hospital administrator confirmed.

Don M., also a hospital administrator, told me that he learned from different health care seminars that "Music therapy works. Not sure of which direction to go for my long-term patients, I decided to start with myself and bought a tape of Baroque medleys. I was excited to discover that my usual short attention span was lengthened with this music. It helped me to concentrate better when reading or studying, as well as drown out outside distractions."

INTERPRETATION: As a result of Don's personal experience with applying music therapy, he has gained insight and a comfort level for suggesting what might work within the hospital. Don is currently developing a program for the hospital, in consultation with a music therapist. I've also talked to many nurses who have, on a day-to-day basis, the closest interaction with patients. The next two statements represent the comments of many.

"While working in the Post Anesthesia Care Unit, I saw the therapeutic effects of music firsthand with patients who requested that they be allowed to wear headphones playing music during surgery and in the immediate post-op period. These patients appeared to experience a calmness and sense of well-being."
—BARBARA NELSON, B.S.N., R.N.

"Music works its wonders on healthy people as well as patients experiencing illness. I have observed the positive effects of reducing stress listening to music. I've also seen music work for patients to the point where healing can be enhanced. In the neonatal intensive care unit, soothing classical music stabilized vital signs for newborns, as well as stabilizing the stress of their parents."
—MICHELE BONNÉE-NICHOLS, R.N., B.S.N., M.A.

INTERPRETATION: Nurses are very open to the application of music as a therapeutic tool once they have seen it work on their patients. Applying music correctly makes their job easier and more rewarding because the patients—and their families—are happier and may heal faster. Following is a dramatic story (from a worried daughter's perspective) about one woman's hospitalization that was cut short with the application of therapeutic music.

"My mother was admitted to the hospital for an angioplasty (repair of blood vessels). She was experiencing a high state of anxiety, even refusing at first to sign the required authorization for possible emergency surgery. Having been so healthy all her life, she didn't know how to handle illness, and a hospital seemed a terrifying place. She didn't think she deserved this.

"Well, the angioplasty catheter balloon burst the artery and immediate double-bypass heart surgery was required. I talked to Judith several days afterward when my mother was stable but still anxiety-ridden and distressed. When Judith asked me what music was being used, I was dismayed, I had forgotten! In all my worry about Mom, I was focusing on nutrition and prayer, but I had forgotten music. Judith asked if my mother liked to listen to music at all (yes) and what she liked to listen to most. I knew right away: Zamfir's pan flutes.

I swooped up tapes and deck and rushed to the hospital. Still overwrought, Mom agreed to listen. I remained with her as long as I could, and I could see Mom, tense even in sleep, gradually relaxing as Zamfir's music continued to play. She was allowed early discharge from the hospital, less than one week after open-heart surgery."

—MARIE T., HOLISTIC PRACTITIONER, MID-FORTIES

INTERPRETATION: An irregular heart rate is normal after open-heart surgery. In this case, however, with entrainment to the music, the regular heart rate resumed within twelve hours instead of the expected two or three days. What I had been able to work through with Marie was a discovery of music to which her mother already had a specific positive conditioning. This frequently makes the initial step with music easier: start with what has proven effectiveness.

If her mother had no favorite Soothing music, we would have had to find another route. Perhaps a brief matching of an Unsettled mood, sequenced to calming music of peace and promise. Or maybe initially trying one of the universal Soothing pieces would have been beneficial, since exhaustion from anxiety might have brought her mother to the point where only Soothing music was needed. Perhaps a sequence of short Unsettling, longer Soothing, and medium-length Energizing music could have been used. What we would not have done was make a hasty decision on "something cheerful" and inflict it on Marie's mother.

Because hospital staff may be too busy to spend a large amount of time addressing patients' individual emotional needs, I recommend that patient care facilities stock inexpensive portable cassette decks and headphones, with a selection of Soothing recordings for patients to USE. (Music channels on hospital-wide TV systems may be available, but are not as effective as using the aforementioned.)

Manuel B., age seventy-five, suffers from chronic depression. He discovered that a sequenced music therapy tape complements the medication his doctor prescribed. "As I listen to the depression-matching music on the tape, something seems to come into my chest, grab the depression, and pull it out physically. The second portion of the tape makes me think of love—'Ave Maria.' I feel much better, at peace."

INTERPRETATION: As discussed in chapter 2, music may increase low levels of the brain chemical that causes depression. To Manuel, this chemical activity felt like his depression was being pulled out of his body. Matching music with love filled him with peace, effectively replacing his depression for a period of time.

"Ave Maria" is not going to work for everyone, but neither will Tina Turner! Respect music as medicine. It is both gentle and powerful, with the ability to shift you out of or into balance. I remind workshop attendees: What stops pain for you may create pain for someone else! This is not meant as a deterrent to helping others, but rather a call for common sense and extra care when recommending music—recommending anything—to others.

A divorced executive, age forty, shared this story: "Music has been invaluable in balancing the emotional health of my family. My wife left me with two sons, ages one and five. I try to be, and think I am, a dedicated, loving father, but it was very stressful raising two energetic boys by myself and, admittedly, my temper exploded once too often. The lack of a mother affected my youngest son the most. Every day was a bad day at day care; he was unable to control his temper tantrums.

"I started going with another woman who loved music and that really influenced me. For work in my office I need to be both calm and energetic. Now, my favorites are Yanni's 'Live at the Acropolis' and the classical tape I made myself. I call it 'Energy,' with Side A slow classical and Side B fast. My younger son picks out his own music, too: Kenny G and even Brahms. Today, I'm remarried, my younger son is eight years old, and both our tempers have cooled. We have learned to communicate with each other again."

INTERPRETATION: Music is successful in relieving ongoing stress when chosen to meet specific emotional needs. Instead of relying solely on the rock music of the '70s, which had initially been the only music he had, this man expanded his collection to include the Japanese instrumental/synthesized works of Kitaro, classical medleys, and Yanni's music. All helped to reduce his daily feelings of frustration. The following story concerns music's healing power when emotional and physical pain overlap.

Jill C., age seventy-two, had been diagnosed as having fibromyalgia, a form of arthritis where pain points reside within muscles. "The kind of all-over pain that's worse than delivering a baby. I couldn't get out of bed, I would fall out of bed. My hands curled and couldn't straighten until they were in a hot wax treatment. I would put elastic on doorknobs so I could open doors with both hands." Music helps her alter her sleep patterns, relaxing her so that she doesn't fall back so quickly into the disturbed sleep that lacks deep REM sleep, typical with fibromyalgia. "Strauss waltzes and Zamfir's pan flute used to work, but now Joan Burns-Miller's 'Sunflower' and 'Desertflower' tapes are the best." As an afterthought, Jill told me that she knows of many arthritis sufferers who are using music for pain relief.

Jill also uses music when she catches herself trying to do too much. "Tony Bennett makes me slow down. You can't rush around when 'I Left My Heart in San Francisco' is playing."

INTERPRETATION: Jill realized that music's ability to manage her pain required her constant vigilance in monitoring its effect on her. Even though the music of Strauss and Zamfir is still applicable, she simply grew tired of hearing these pieces after constant playing, and sought new music for relaxation. She discovered she liked music with added nature sounds, so she might also like "Cool Mountain Stream" by Platinum Disc Corp., which in a recent study produced significant reduction in anxiety, thus promoting relaxation for preoperative patients.[6] The next step for her might be entrainment recordings that produce deep relaxation states.

Fifty years younger than Jill, Jenny R. is not in physical pain but is equally interested in coping skills. Living with her parents in New York to save on finances, Jenny relies on the intensity levels of the music of Led Zeppelin and Beethoven to help her vent a bad mood rather than taking it out on those at home. She might also consider "Heal Me" by Gwen Mars, Mahavishnu Orchestra's "Wings of Karma," Berlioz's "Dream of a Sabbath Night," or "Pruit Igoe" from the soundtrack of the film "Koyaanisqatsi."

A sequence to Soothing, then Energizing, music could help her achieve the cathartic experience.

Several intensity levels up from Jenny, a constant rage had been running the life of Kristine L., also in her twenties, who had a childhood rife with severe domestic violence. Consequently, her relationships with everyone—friends, strangers, and husband—were seriously affected. She never went anywhere by herself and she always worried about whether people would accept her. She knew karate well enough to hurt people, but could not maintain good control, thus she seriously injured a girlfriend during a workout. This increased her fear of people, as she worried about what she might be prompted to do to them. When I met her, her home had become her prison.

Music therapy included counseling sessions and a specialized tape I had developed. Kristine said that at first she had problems listening to the music that evoked love, because it brought up too many bad recollections. "Nobody in my family loved me and it upset me to try and experience love because I didn't know how to feel it, and I wanted to so badly. So I was relieved when the tape player broke! Then, I realized that I really did need to listen to that kind of music because I was starting to feel better. So I got the stereo system fixed and made myself listen to it religiously—at least once a day.

"I used to be scared of people, and in less than two months I was able to smile and even talk to strangers. I've set up my own business, gotten the necessary contracts to secure business through the next three years, and started back to work. Music, lots of new and different music, has become a very important element in my life now. *Enigma* even brought sex back to my marriage!"

Although it seems hard to believe that anyone could have a problem listening to music of love, I've heard this before. And, I'm not surprised when one loves Unsettling music that could make another cringe. The effects of individuality are compounded by any one person's physiological responses to the various elements of music. It is this combination that creates your musical favorites and the music that can help heal you.

All the techniques, observations, and stories shared here have been directed toward identifying the best way for you to put together a range of music you can reach for in times of pain or problems. This program for USEing music has a fundamental requirement—that you take personal responsibility for your own well-being. That commitment to yourself, plus the healing power of music, can be an unbeatable combination.

12

Refrain and Finale

A GOOD REFRAIN will repeat a song's emotional theme, and we have looked at many themes, in terms of musical analysis, emotional analysis, and the correlation of one to the other. The length and breadth of your emotional potential is awe-inspiring. But you cannot begin to control your emotions, if that is what you want, or begin to experience them fully and clearly, if that is what you want, or do both well, if that is what you want, without reducing their complexity to some manageable level. It is important to put your emotions into context, juxtaposed against the realities of your daily lives and loves. Put them into context, as well, within the experience of physical pain. Emotions can be causes, accompanists to, and results of, physical pain. That is the emotionality of the patterns of pain.

The many avenues of psychiatric and psychological counseling—prayer, meditation, spiritual counseling, medical intervention, physical stress-relief procedures, holistic techniques, appropriate medication, and behavior modification—are all available. Music provides another avenue, one that most of us don't fully appreciate. USE your music to get where you want to go, to find the inner place of the self at peace.

Emotional Comfort Levels

You seek relief from pain and you seek your emotional, peaceful center. Some of you would also like to achieve a peaceful center with excitement around the edges. Inner peace, fresh energy, and healthy emotional control—these are important, substantive goals. Let's add another: emotional fluidity, your ability to fluently experience a broad range of emotions. I believe that not only centering, but your ability to get "unstuck," to be emotionally mobile, is crucial to a positive state of wellness.

Stress and pain are bad enough in themselves and, certainly, the situation worsens if they take over your life. To stress and pain, you then add a focus on stress and pain, and a circle of self-defeat has begun. Goals will stay out of reach. Your self-image will be affected, which in turn affects your ability to function in relationships at home, work, in all forms of social interactions, and in your own health maintenance.

Sometimes, emotions seem to control our lives. We all know people who act out their anger. We all know people who need to live on love. We all know people who will never take a risk. Some of us are trapped in one set of feelings, emotionally congealed, because of severely traumatic experiences. Constant pain, physically experienced, also has tremendous emotional consequences and holds the sufferer in emotional as well as physical bondage.

Emotions can also control your life if you are wrongly controlling them. If you're limiting your emotional expression because you are scared, withdrawn, or just determinedly better-mannered than the rest of us folks, you build your own cage. Deepak Chopra, M.D., expressed this eloquently:

> *As adults, when we deny ourselves the immediate experience of an emotion, a screen of words is put up by the mind and this throws us out of the present and into either the past or the future. To feel an emotion fully and completely, to experience it and then release it is to be in the present, the only moment that never ages.*[1]

Any kind of emotional imbalance, for whatever reason, will have a direct effect on your health. I am not only speaking of pain here, but of the total expression of good health. You need to allow both harmony and conflict in your life. You need to express a range of emotions for your full health potential, moving cleanly from one emotion to another, and you need to face any negative emotion, whatever the cause—not repressing it, not intending to think about it tomorrow, but accepting it now. Then bring music into play, literally.

Not every single emotion of which a human being is capable will correspond to the three categories we are considering: Unsettled, Soothed, and Energized. But the majority of emotions will fall into these categories, including those that interact with pain. I expect that among them you will find the prime activators of your daily life. In your quest to change moods, alleviate pain, enhance creative efforts, or fully express yourself, do you have the music corollaries to help you achieve your goals? If your collection already includes the selections highlighted in the previous chapters, you have a head start on the USE of music for healing.

You may have been USEing music to healthful effect all along, without ever being fully aware of it. I am a major advocate for trusting your intuition. Your intuition communicates with you every minute of every day and night. When you are tuned in, you know exactly how to express your feelings—about anything— simply and directly, without residual thoughts or feelings, so you may have been reaching automatically, without thinking twice about it, for the right music. Now you will be able to back up that deep-seated awareness with specific knowledge.

Remember the components of our method:

The correct music   **Unsettling** *if you need to match emotional pain.*

Soothing *as a transition, to initiate relief from emotional or physical pain, and as a total calming experience.*

Energizing *for an infusion of joy and vitality.*

at the right moment. . .in the best sequence.

Music Comfort Levels

As you start to work with music related to your emotional needs, begin with what you know, your favorite music style or performer(s).

As a first step, when a favorite style is your primary focus, try adjusting the music element of *intensity*, the simple dynamics of soft versus loud, to attain different emotions, for example, soft for relaxation and settling in to sleep, loud for energy.

Most listeners will find some emotions in all three categories within a favorite style. To use rock as an example, you can work with all variants. Alternative, including grunge and industrial, tends to match Unsettling moods. Trance (aka ambient techno) usually matches Soothing moods. Techno, house, and hip-hop are Energizers. Classic rock pieces could be found in all three USE categories. Any single style may have certain mood limitations, containing all three categories but being primarily Unsettling, Soothing, or Energizing. Experiment, both within a favorite style, and with styles new to you, to discover what you will listen to without grimacing, and what will supply the necessary range of emotions for your healing program.

Solo artists and groups work hard to develop signature sounds and, in many cases, signature mood textures as well. USE their music for the one category or single mood, then find recordings by other performers for the balance of a mood-matching sequence. On many albums, artists will play around a bit with different sounds to give the album greater interest and, by doing so, provide you with a variety of musical moods. Again, this is a route for discovery, fascinating and occasionally frustrating.

Both with favorite artists and favorite music, if you find you are listening to music that provides a limited area of emotions, I encourage you to broaden your tastes. Cross over to other music, to "fill in the cracks" of your emotional range and to better your health. Here is an example of what you might accomplish with music:

SADNESS INTO PEACE

Consider listening to music from the blues, soul, soundtrack, popular, or classical styles to match moods of sadness. Then change to new age, Christian, classical, or world music to match peaceful emotions.

LETHARGY INTO ENERGY

Consider listening to music from new age, classical or easy listening categories to match feelings of tiredness. Then change to music from new age, classical, country, classic, or techno rock, R & B, gospel, world, or big band styles to match high-energy levels.

FRUSTRATION INTO ACCEPTANCE

Consider listening to music from jazz, classical, rap, industrial or alternative styles to match moods of frustration or anger. Then change to music from new age, gospel, Christian, popular, easy listening, trance (rock), or world to match moods of acceptance.

PAIN INTO RELIEF

Consider implementing Guided Imagery & Music (GIM), a successful pain-relief method, which involves using the full Unsettling-Soothing-Energizing sequence, working with a qualified music therapist. On your own, you can also work with familiar Soothing and Energizing music to break pain patterns.

> *Emotional exclusivity: It is impossible to feel two emotions at once. Pick music in any style that brings forth for you emotions of peace or joy, to void such emotions as anxiety, fear, anger, and despair that are part of pain's grim hold.*

> *Muscle relaxation: With anger, fear, and anxiety come angry, tense muscles. Muscle tension tends to feed on itself, the tension causing more tension, in a vicious circle. Muscle tension that accompanies pain can be helped with music-assisted relaxation techniques.*

> *Electrochemical activity: Music relates to the effectiveness of the body's natural pain-relief mechanisms. Music that is sequenced to alleviate depression and other pain-related emotions can be a factor in pain relief.*

All styles can be USEd successfully. I have found that favorite, familiar music is often the best. It comes as a friend, and pain is a lonely place.

Helping Others

Some of you were led to this book to help a friend or a family member who is ill, confined at home, in a hospice, or in a health care facility. I encourage you to both bring music to them and to give some thoughtful consideration to what music will be right for that individual. Think about the emotional variants within unsettled, soothed, or energized conditions, and the corresponding Unsettling, Soothing, and Energizing music selections. For someone who is ill it is particularly crucial that you become sensitive to their true condition and what might help them. Give a great deal of credence to your intuition in this matter, remembering that the part of your mind that goes beyond logic is capable of surprisingly accurate analysis.

> A woman who had trauma to her leg had surgery. After the surgery, for some reason, her leg simply did not work. This went on for weeks, months. Finally, the neurologist said to her, "Since you have been hurt, can you ever think of a time when your leg has moved?" The woman thought and she said, "Yes, on one occasion, I remember I heard on a radio station an Irish jig being played. And I remembered the days of my youth and my leg involuntarily moved.' As a result, the doctor, recognizing that her leg would move under certain conditions, began a program of music therapy, playing Irish music.
>
> Now, this day, the woman is normal. They were able to reestablish full use of that limb. There are many cases like that that cost no money [Author's note: not quite 'no,' but less money, certainly.] It got her out of a wheelchair.
>
> —Senator Harry Reid, D-Nev. Congressional Record, 137, 129.

Employ whichever avenue or avenues are open. Ask the person directly, question people close to them, or personally observe them if that is possible. (If a music therapist is available, that's even better.) Combine your self-awareness and sensitivity to others with the healing capabilities inherent in music. Then you will bring the sound of healing as a message of hope and help, as a token of your own loving care, which is a message in itself.

If you are interested in this extended aspect of music and healing, I think you'll appreciate the following story about two sisters who shared a hospital vigil:

Beth:
"My mother was always a strong, independent, intelligent woman. Consequently, my family and I were not prepared for the suddenness of what happened [her aneurysm, brain hemorrhage, and three-month hospital stay] and certainly not prepared for the life of a hospital's intensive care unit. The smells, the sounds of all the machines, the groans of patients, were all foreign to me. My sister was there the first week."

Mari:
"My sister and brothers and I took turns staying at her bedside providing company and reassuring her when she became confused. It was often difficult to shut out the disturbances of the hospital setting, and Mom reacted to the noises with disorientation and agitation. As the hours extended into days and then weeks, I sought the medium of music as a setting for peace and healing in the midst of the hospital distractions, so I bought a radio/cassette player for her room. Initially, I played my own current favorites, mostly new age, but I found that these were less relaxing for Mom. The musical selections that reached her were those that imparted a gentle familiarity, particularly the melodious classical music she loved. My sister followed my turn with Mom and continued to use music."

Beth:
"When I arrived for my three-week stay, I continued what my sister had started, and I bought some additional tapes. One of them, my favorite, was Pachelbel's 'Canon,' with ocean sounds. She knew and loved this music. As I played a variety of music for my mother, this one piece became the one that seemed to soothe her the most."

Mari:
"Then, Mom suffered a stroke, totally disorienting her and leading into the most critical part of her hospitalization. Even in the intensive care unit, my sister continued playing music through

headphones to relieve Mom's agitation. She eventually found that she could calm Mom more effectively than with any medicine by repetitively playing the Pachelbel 'Canon.' With time, our mother recovered. I know that the therapeutic effect of music was a major part of survival and healing."

—BETH DUNCOMBE, ELEMENTARY SCHOOL PRINCIPAL
—MARI DUNCOMBE KOCH, M.D.

The Sound of Healing

Pachelbel's music, melodious classical music in general, or any one style may or may not be the right choice for you in a particular situation because of the personal differences element in music therapy. But somewhere, for everyone, there is a style of music that will do the healing work. To return to a theme from chapter 1: Unity lies in music's ability to heal, diversity lies in our individual ways of finding our own healing levels.

Given that diversity, it's my expectation that this book will be used differently by different people. It is, in part, a buying guide to music, an aid to better organization of a music collection, a philosophical treatise, a music analysis reference, and an examination of the undercurrents in human lives. I believe you can keep coming back to it, just as I believe you will keep returning to music for both pleasure and a powerful healing experience. I was raised to love music; I have learned to appreciate and apply its true power; and I wish you the best of all of these experiences.

Chapter 7/8: Music That UNSETTLES

Emotion	Style	Music Selection (Sounds like/crosses over to. . .)	Artist and/or Composer
SADNESS	Country	"Thunder Rolls" from *No Fences* and *The Hits* (New Country)	Garth Brooks
	Rap	"I Seen a Man Die" from *The Diary*	Scarface
GRIEF	Popular	"The Rose"	Amanda McBroom
MOURNFULNESS	Soul	"Pearls" from *Best of Sade*	Sade
	Classical	"Lento Sostenuto" from "Symphony No. 3, Opus 36"	Henryck Gorecki
DEPRESSION	Rock	"Perfect Blue Buildings" from *August & Everything After* (Alter.)	Counting Crows
	Classical	"Funeral March" from "Sonata No. 2, Op. 35"	Frederic Chopin
	Rock	"Mercy Street" from *So*	Peter Gabriel
	Rock	"I Want You" from *Abbey Road* (Rock 'n' Roll)	Beatles
ANXIETY	Classical	"Mars, the Bringer of War" from "The Planets"	Gustav Holst
	New Age	"Festival of Crows" from *Poems of the Five Mountains*	Timmerman & Wise
	Classical	"Inferno Dance" from "Firebird Suite, Part I"	Igor Stravinsky
ANGER	Jazz	"Wings of Karma" from *Apocalypse* (Rock)	Mahavishnu Orchestra
	Film	"Pruit Igoe" from "Koyaanisqatsi"	Philip Glass
	Classical	"Dream of a Sabbath Night" from "Symphonie Fantastique"	Hector Berlioz
FEAR	Classical	"Allegro" from "Symphony No. 10 in E minor"	Dmitri Shostakovich

- Tape/CD/Album titles are italicized.
- The music is found under the style, but ("Sounds like/crosses over to . . .) does sound like something else.

Chapter 7/9: Music That SOOTHES

Emotion	Style	Music Selection (Sounds like. . .)	Artist and/or Composer
SENTIMENTALITY	Jazz	"Sentimental" from *Breathless*	Kenny G
	Classical	"Ballad Theme" from "Rhapsody in Blue" (Jazz)	George Gershwin
	Easy Listening	"Unforgettable" from *Unforgettable*	Natalie Cole
TENDERNESS	Stage	"The Music of the Night" from "Phantom of the Opera"	Andrew Lloyd Webber
	Film	"Evergreen" from "A Star Is Born" (Popular)	Barbra Streisand
	New Age	"The Cello's Song" from *A Childhood Remembered*	Kostia and David Arkenstone
SERENITY	Classical	"Liebestraum No. 3"	Franz Liszt
CALMNESS	New Age	"Mysterious Island" from *Planet Drum* (World)	Mickey Hart
	Classical	"Fantasia on Greensleeves"	Ralph Vaughan Williams
	New Age	"Forever" from *The Edge of Forever*	Hilary Stagg
TRANQUILITY	Classical	*Chant* (Gregorian)	Benedictine Monks of SDDS
	New Age	"Healing Dance" from *Music to Disappear in II* (World)	Raphael
RELAXATION	Classical	"Canon in D Major"	Johann Pachelbel
	Classical	"Largo" from "Winter" of "The Four Seasons"	Antonio Vivaldi
	New Age	"Song of the Seashore" from *Song of the Seashore and other Melodies of Japan* (World)	Narita
	New Age	"Fogflute" from *Isle of Skye*	Jeffrey Thompson, D. C.

Chapter 7/10: Music That ENERGIZES

Emotion	Style	Music Selection (Sounds like. . .)	Artist and/or Composer
EXHILARATION	Rock	"Let the Beat Control Your Body" from *No Limits* (Techno)	2 Unlimited
	Country	"Orange Blossom Special" from *The New Nashville Cats*	Mark O'Connor
	Classical	"William Tell Overture"	Gioacchino Rossini
CHEERFULNESS	Jazz	"Practice Makes Perfect" from *Dragonfly Summer*	Michael Franks
	New Age	"Celestial Soda Pop" from *Deep Breakfast*	Ray Lynch
	Jazz	"In the Mood" (Big Band)	Glenn Miller
	World	"Brazil" from *Fiesta*	A. Barroso/Cincinnati Pops
JOYOUSNESS	Classical	"Espana"	Emmanuel Chabrier
	New Age	"Odessa" from *The Sacred Fire*	Nicholas Gunn
	Classical	"Hallelujah Chorus" from the "Messiah"	George F. Handel
LIGHT-HEARTEDNESS	Film	"The Circle of Life" from "The Lion King" (World)	Elton John
	Classical	"On the Beautiful Blue Danube"	Johannn Strauss, Jr.
ENTHUSIASM	Popular	"Emotions" from *Emotions*	Mariah Carey
	Classical	"Presto" from "Symphony No. 35 in D major—Haffner"	Wolfgang Amadeus Mozart
	New Age	"Swept Away" from *Live at the Acropolis* (Jazz)	Yanni
	Classical	"Presto" from "Symphony No. 7 in A major"	Ludwig von Beethoven

Additional USE Music List: UNSETTLING

Emotion	Style	Music Selection (Sounds like. .)	Artist and/or Composer
SADNESS	Blues	"House of the Rising Sun" from *Jazz, Ballards & Blues*	Josh White Jr. & Robin Batteau
GRIEF	Classical	"Adagio Lamentoso" from "Symphony No. 6 - Pathetique"	Peter Tchaikovsky
	Classical	"Primo Tempore" from *Officium* (Gregorian, Jazz)	J. Garbarek/Hilliard Ensemble
DEPRESSION	Country	"Outside Myself" from *Ingenue* (Pop/Folk)	k.d. lang
AGONY	Popular	"Pain Revisited" from *What Silence Knows*	Shara Nelson
ANXIETY	Classical	"Sinfonietta, Op. 60"	Leos Janacek
	Classical	"Ride of the Valkyries"	Richard Wagner
ANGER	Film	"Betrayal and Desolation" from "Braveheart" (Classical)	James Horner
	Rock	"Heal Me" from *Magnosheen*	Gwen Mars
	Film	"The Battle on the Ice" from "Alexander Nevsky Cantata, Op. 78"	Sergei Prokofiev

Additional USE Music: SOOTHING

Emotion	Style	Music Selection	Artist and/or Composer
TENDERNESS	Country	"You Can Sleep While I Drive" from *Thinkin About You*	Trisha Yearwood
	Opera	"O mio babbino caro" from "Gianni Schicchi"	Giacomo Puccini
REVERENCE	Christian	"I've Just Seen Jesus" from *Instrument of Praise*	Phil Driscoll
CALMNESS	Rock	"Windwind" from *Incunabula* (Trance)	Autechre
	New Age	*Fairy Ring*	Mike Rowland
TRANQUILITY	New Age	*Equinox*	Jean Michel Jarre
	New Age	"Cool Mountain Stream" from *Relaxation Series* (Environ.)	Platinum Disc Corp.
RELAXATION	Classical	"Adagio" from "Organ Symphony in C# minor"	Camille Saint-Saens
	Classical	"Clair de Lune"	Claude Debussy
	Classical	"Air on the G String"	Johann S. Bach

Additional USE Music: ENERGIZING

Emotion	Style	Music Selection	Artist and/or Composer
EXHILARATION	Gospel	"Hallelujah" from *Black Gospel Explosion*	The Clark Sisters
	Zydeco	"Jeunes Filles de Quatorze Ans" from *La Danse de la Vie*	BeauSoleil
	Classical	"Stars and Stripes Forever"	John P. Sousa
LIGHT-HEARTEDNESS	New Age	"Orinoco Flow" from *Watermark*	Enya
	Jazz	"The Entertainer" (Ragtime)	Scott Joplin
CHEERFULNESS	Rock	"Soul Shakedown Party" from *At His Best* (Reggae)	Bob Marley
	Opera	"La donna e mobile" from "Rigoletto"	Giuseppe Verdi
JOYOUSNESS	New Age	"Just One World" from *Acoustic Planet* (New Country)	Craig Chaquico
	Jazz	"Dis Is Da Drum" from *Dis Is Da Drum*	Herbie Hancock
ENTHUSIASM	New Age	"Fire From the Sky" from *The Art of Nature*	Michael Gettel

APPENDIX B: Music USEd in Therapeutic Processes

Two examples of Judith Pinkerton's therapeutic music products, analyzed in their USE categories, follow:

Mildly Energizing to Soothing

Music Selection: MEE (Music Exercising Emotions™) in the Key of Peace (52:28)

Composers: Various, including Strauss, Brahms, Schubert, Schumann, Bach, Tchaikovsky, Mendelssohn, and traditional folk songs

Instrumentation: Solo violin

Commentary: Thirty-three solo violin selections were chosen, the result of the original tape USEd for my husband while in the hospital, and dozens of personal performances during which audiences were asked what they wanted to hear. All are potentially Soothing choices and several have been reported by music therapist researchers as eliciting a state of relaxation, for example, Brahm's "Lullaby," Saint-Saens' "The Swan," Schubert's "Serenade" and "Ave Maria."[1]

The selections have been sequenced to appear as nonstop playing. Tempos express overalertness at the beginning, moving into a relaxed or drowsy state by the end. For your reference, the thirty-three selections, in order, are:

"On the Beautiful Blue Danube"
   by Strauss
"Carnival of Venice" by Ambrosio
"Schon Rosmarin" by Kreisler
"Scheherezade" by Rimsky-Korsakov
"Preludio in E major" by Bach
"Gavotte en Rondeau" by Bach
"Loure" by Bach
"Humoresque" by Dvorak
"Hungarian Dance #5" by Brahms
"Hungarian Rhapsody #2" by Liszt
"Habanera" from "Carmen" by Bizet
"La Cumparsita" (Spanish traditional)
"Cadenza" from "Violin Concerto in
   G major" by Mozart
"Serenade" by Haydn
"La Cinquintaine" by Gabriel-Marie
"Serenade" by Schubert
"Canzonetta" by Tchaikovsky
"Greensleeves" (English traditional)

"Adagio in G minor" by Bach
"Passacaglia" by Von Biber
"Hatikvoh" (Hebrew traditional)
"Danny Boy" or "Londonderry Air"
   (Irish traditional)
"Souvenir de Moscow"
   by Wieniawski
"Drink to Me Only with Thine Eyes"
   (English traditional)
"The Swan" by Saint-Saens
"Pavane" by Ravel
"Traumerei" by Schumann
"Andante" from "Violin Concerto
   in E minor" by Mendelssohn
"Ave Maria" by Schubert
"Ave Maria" by Bach-Gounod
"Shenandoah" (Traditional)
"Home Sweet Home" by Bishop
"Lullaby" by Brahms

Unsettling through Soothing to Energizing

Music Selection: MEE (Music Exercising Emotions™) Concert (24:16)
Composers: Judith Pinkerton, Alan MacIntosh
Instrumentation: Violin, piano, synthesizers, electric/acoustic bass, drums
Commentary: This concert was developed over a two-year period. Individual pieces were initially played with a variety of musicians, based on positive audience response regarding the emotions evoked. Alan MacIntosh did the arrangements for a five-piece band and composed two additional original pieces. These arrangements were based on the principles of Sentic Cycles research, which theorizes that experiencing a broad emotional range in a sequence may aid the healing process.[2] Sentic Cycles, developed by neuroscientist Dr. Manfred Clynes, established one format for emotional sequencing.

The MEE Concert enables the listener to journey through four music sections, "Angst, Drone, Love, and Joy," to evoke four different emotional states, from two stages of Unsettled through Soothed to Energized.

"Angst" has a quick tempo and pitch successions, which are deliberately designed to evoke anxiety and fear. The music is an arrangement of Henri Sauguet's "La Rue Tourne," followed by Jacques Ibert's "Entr'Acte" with a section from Bela Bartok's "First Rhapsody."

"Drone" is next, an original piece that simulates a state of depression with a fusion of classical and jazz music. The bass and violin intentionally avoid using vibrato to omit heart-tugging intensity.

"Love" follows with a dramatic transition that triggers an emotional release (many cry!). This music section is an arrangement of two classical works, "Ave Maria" by Bach-Gounod and "Recuerdos de la Alhambra" by Francisco Tarrega. Two emotion-charged elements are featured: the tremolo technique of gypsy flamenco and the violin's fast vibrato.

"Joy" highlights an original music piece called "Steel Feel" in the world (reggae) style, succeeded by Scott Joplin's "The Entertainer," perhaps best known as the theme music for the movie "The Sting." "Steel Feel" opens with an anapestic beat (short-short-long) to get the listener moving into a livelier mood. All the instruments improvise solos on the catchy, happy melody.

Both of these are examples of sequencing music—and from the music, your own emotions.

APPENDIX C: Resources

Organizations:
The purpose of the resource organizations listed below is to promote the scientific use of therapeutically applied music through qualified music therapists, public education, degree programs, research validation, and products:

For certified music therapists and music therapy degree programs:
American Association for Music Therapy, Inc.
One Station Plaza, Ossining, NY 10562
(914) 944-9260

For registered music therapists and music therapy degree programs:
National Association for Music Therapy, Inc.
8455 Colesville Road, Suite 930, Silver Spring, MD 20910
(301) 589-3300

For more information on LIND (Learning In New Dimensions) music for accelerated learning and stress reduction:
The LIND Institute
P.O. Box 14487, San Francisco, CA 94114–0487
(415) 864-3396 or 1-800 462-3766

For more information and training in Guided Imagery & Music (GIM) for pain management:
The Bonny Foundation
2020 Simmons, Salina, KS 67401
(913) 827-1497

For Judith Pinkerton's therapeutic music products:
SeminarConcerts™ International
2756 N. Green Valley Pkwy. Suite 88, Green Valley, NV 89014–2120
Tel: (702) 363-8166

For Judith Pinkerton's music therapy workshops:
The Center for Creative Therapeutic Arts
2756 N. Green Valley Pkwy. Suite 88, Green Valley, NV 89014–2120
Tel: (702) 363-8166

I am indebted to the following authors for general information and supportive materials:

Bonny, H., and L. Savary (1973). *Music and your mind: listening with a new consciousness.* Harper & Row.

Bressler, D. (1979). *Free yourself from pain.* Simon and Schuster.

Clynes. M. (1982). *Music, mind and brain: the neuropsychology of music.* Plenum Press.

Critchley, M. (1977). *Music and the brain: studies in the neurology of music.* Heinemann Medical Books.

Gross, and Swartz (1982). *The effects of music therapy on anxiety in chronically ill patients.* Journal for the American Association of Music Therapy, 2 (1), 43–52.

Hodges, D. (1980). *Handbook of music psychology.* National Association for Music Therapy, Inc.

Lingerman, H.A. (1983). *The healing energies of music*. Theosophical Publishing House.

Locsin, R. (1981). *The effect of music on the pain of selected postoperative patients*. Journal of Advanced Nursing, 6 (19).

Maranto, C. (1991). *Applications of music in medicine*. National Association for Music Therapy, Inc.

Marcus, N. (1994). *Freedom from chronic pain*. Simon & Schuster.

Pickett, E. (1994). Journal of the association for music and imagery. The Bonny Foundation, Vol. 3.

Pinkerton, J. (1993). Music: the stress-release system in 3 steps. Seminar Concerts International.

Ratner, L.G. (1983). *The musical experience*. W.H. Freeman and Co.

Rider, M. (1985). *Entrainment mechanisms are involved in pain reduction, muscle relaxation and music-mediated imagery*. Journal of Music Therapy, XXII, (4), 183–192.

Rider, M.S. and C.T. Eagle, Jr. (1986). *Rhythmic entrainment as a mechanism for learning in music therapy*, in *Rhythm in psychological, linguistic and musical processes*. Charles C. Thomas, 226–242.

NOTES

Chapter 1
1. Clynes, M., and N. Nettheim (1982). *The living quality of music: neurobiologic patterns of communicating feeling*, in *Music, Mind and Brain*. Plenum Press, 52.
2. Blakeslee, S. *The mystery of music: how it works in the brain*. The New York Times, May 16, 1995.
3. Clynes, M., and N. Nettheim (1982). Op cit.
4. Bonny, H. (1981). *Music and sound in health*, in Hastings, Fadiman, and Gordon, *Health for the whole person*. Westview Press.
5. Goldberg, J. *Music as medicine*. McCall's, January 1987, Vol. 114, 105.

Chapter 2
1. Altschuler, J. (1948). *A psychiatrist's experiences with music as a therapeutic agent*, in Schullian and Schoer (eds.) *Music and medicine*, Henry Schulman, Inc.
2. Hall, M. (1982). *The therapeutic value of music, including the philosophy of music.* Philosophical Research Society, 19–20.
3. Atwater, F.H. (1989). *The physics of entrainment*, in *Hemisync process: a theoretical perspective*. The Monroe Institute, 1–8.
4. Leonard, G. (1986). *The silent pulse*. E.P. Dutton, 15.
5. Flaherty, T. (1993). *Mind and brain.* Time Life Books, 72; and Rauscher, F., Shaw, G., Levine, L., Ky, K. and E. Wright (1994). *Music and spatial task performance: a causal relationship.* University of California, Irvine, and Irvine Conservatory of Music.
6. Di Franco, J. (1988). *Relaxation: music*, in Nichols & Humenick's *Childbirth education, practice, research and theory.* Saunders, 207.
7. Staum, M., and M. Brotons. (1992). *The influence of auditory subliminals on behavior: a series of investigations.* The Journal of Music Therapy, XXIX, (3), 139.
8. Short, A. (1992). *Music and imagery with physically disabled elderly residents: a GIM adaptation.* Music Therapy, 11, (1), 65–98.
9. Goldberg, J. Op cit.
10. Lee, M. *Forever young: music and aging.* Testimony to U.S. Senate Special Committee on Aging Conference, August 1, 1991.
11. Sacks, O. (1990). *Awakenings.* Harper Perrenial, xiii, 60.
12. Pierce, J.R. (1983). *The science of musical sound.* Scientific American Books, Inc., 21.
13. Schulberg, C. (1981). *The music therapy sourcebook: a collection of activities.* Human Sciences Press, 18–21.
14. Sachs, C. (1953). *Rhythm and tempo.* W.W. Norton & Co., NY, 21–2.
15. Scarantino, B. (1987). *Music power.* Dodd, Mead and Co., 33.
16. Brody, R. *Which music helps your muscles?* American Health, Jan/Feb, 1988.
17. Franz, F. (1947). *Metronome techniques.* Franz, 12.
18. Sachs, C. (1953). Op cit.
19. Brecker, E. (1994). *Schindler's legacy.* Plume Book, 12.
20. Tames, D. (1984). *The secret power of music.* Destiny Books, 110.
21. Schulberg, C. (1981). Op cit, 46–8.

Chapter 3
1. Buch, D. *Listeners do not want limits.* Letter to the editor, Billboard, April 22, 1995, 4.
2. Mannes, G. *Bang on the ROM all day.* Entertainment Weekly, January 27, 1995.

Chapter 4
1. Berfume, D., Fitzpatrick, D., and D. Collins (1979). *History of contemporary music: rock, pop, and jazz.* Radio broadcast for Foothills Community College course.
2. Sachs, C. (1953). *Rhythm and tempo.* W.W. Norton & Co., NY, 370.
3. Hirshey, G. (1984). Op cit, 28.
4. Hirshey, G. (1984). Ibid., 228.
5. Hirshey, G. (1984). Ibid., 298, 305.
6. Vieth, V. *He walks the line.* ABA Journal, May, 1995.

7. Berfume, D., Fitzpatrick, D., and D. Collins (1979). Op cit.

8. *Striving for excellence* (1989). Institute in Basic Life Principles, 48–9.

Chapter 5

1. Ardley, N. (1986). *Music, an illustrated encyclopedia.* Facts on File Inc., 114.

2. Conroy, F. *Stop nitpicking a genius.* The New York Times Magazine, June 25, 1995, 31.

3. Weatherford, M. *Violent dancing.* Las Vegas Review-Journal/Sun., Oct. 14, 1990.

4. Discussion with many rock fans.

5. Discussion with many rock fans.

6. *The ten that matter most 1985–1995.* Spin, April 1995.

7. *Two alternatives to grunge's angst.* The New York Times, March 19, 1995.

8. Rose, T. (1994). *Black noise: rap music and black culture in contemporary America.* Wesleyan University Press, 67–70.

9. Discussion with rap fans.

10. Seib, G. *Time Warner is assailed by Sen. Dole for sex and violence in entertainment.* The Wall Street Journal, June 1, 1995.

11. Shapiro, E., and J. Trachtenberg. *Ads denounce Time Warner for rap music.* The Wall Street Journal, May 17, 1995.

12. Stuessy, J. (1994). *Rock and roll: its history and stylistic development.* Prentice Hall, 409.

Chapter 6

1. Ardley, N. (1986). Op cit, 102–3.

2. Stuessy, J. (1994). Op cit, 364–6.

3. Borzillo, C. *Warren drives a hit-writing machine.* Billboard, April 22, 1995.

4. White, K. *Muzak moves out of the elevator, into the '90s with new formats.* Las Vegas Review Journal, Oct. 28, 1990.

5. *Bach reduces the barking.* Parade Magazine, November 4, 1990, 9.

6. Rauscher, F., Shaw, G., Levine, L., Ky, K. and E. Wright (1994). Op cit.

7. Ostrander, S. and L. Schroeder. (1979). *Superlearning.* Laurel, 115.

8. Campbell, M. *Musicians forsake atonal style.* Associated Press, Las Vegas Review-Journal, Sept. 6, 1992.

9. Tames, D. (1984). op.cit, 94–5.

10. Watson, A. and N. Drury (1987). *Healing music.* Nature and Health Books, 50.

11. Peschel, E. and R. Peschel. *Donizetti and the music of mental derangement: Anna Bolena, Lucia di Lammermoor, and the composer's neurobiological illness.* Yale Journal of Biological Medicine, May-June 1992, 65(3), 189–200.

12. Wilson, E. *Authors' rights in the superhighway era.* Wall Street Journal, Jan. 25, 1995.

13. Watson, A. and N. Drury (1987). Op cit, 79–80.

14. Watson, A. and N. Drury (1987). Ibid., 81.

15. Monmaney, T. *Key notes on the mind.* Omni, January, 1987, 67.

16. Andersen, O. (1993). *The LIND lists: a resource guide and journal.* The LIND Institute, 121.

Chapter 7

1. Ewen, D. (1962). *Popular American Composers.* H.W. Wilson Company, 70.

2. Ewen, D. (1962). Ibid, 70.

3. Ewen, D. (1962). Ibid, 69.

4. Music Research Foundation (1952). *Music and your emotions.* Liveright Publishing, 74.

5. Cross, M. and D. Ewen (1962). *Encyclopedia of the great composers and their music.* Doubleday & Co., 642.

6. Arnold, D. (1983). *The new Oxford companion to music.* Oxford University Press, 1, 342.

Chapter 8

1. Santoro, G. (1974). Printed insert commentary for Mahavishnu Orchestra's *Apocalypse.* Sony Music Entertainment.

2. Ramos, L. (1993). *The effects of on-hold telephone music on the number of premature disconnections to a statewide protective services abuse hot line.* Journal of Music Therapy, 30(2), 119–129.
3. Music Research Foundation, Inc. (1952). Op cit, 72.

Chapter 9
1. Gorelick, K. (1992). Printed insert for *Breathless*. Arista Records.
2. Hart, M. *Forever young: music and aging.* Testimony to U. S. Senate Special Committee on Aging, August 1, 1991.
3. Dyer, R. (1986). *The kind of music lovers love.* Printed insert for Boston Pops compact disc *Pops in Love*. Phillips, West Germany.
4. Foil, D. (1994). Printed insert for *Chant*. Angel Records.
5. Di Franco, J. (1988). Op cit, 213.

Chapter 11
1. Darrow, A., Johnson, C. and T. Ollenberger (1994). *The effect of participation in an intergenerational choir on teens' and older persons' cross-age attitudes.* Journal of Music Therapy, XXXI, (2), 119–134.
2. Clynes, M., and N. Nettheim (1982). Op cit.
3. Schmit, J. *Aging business titans: addicted to the deal.* USA Today, April 13, 1995.
4. The New York Times Magazine, Nov. 20, 1977, 49.
5. Chase, W. *Forever young: music and aging.* Testimony to U. S. Senate Special Committee on Aging Conference, August 1, 1991.
6. Robb, S., Nichols, R., Rutan, R., Bishop, B., and J. Parker (1995). *The effects of music assisted relaxation on preoperative anxiety.* Journal of Music Therapy, XXXII (1), 2–21.

Chapter 12
1. Chopra, Deepak (1993). *Ageless Body, Timeless Mind.* Harmony Books, 186.

Appendix B (Music USEd in Therapeutic Processes)
1. Music Research Foundation., Inc. (1952). Op cit, 123–4.
2. Clynes & Panskepp (1988). *Generalized emotions—how it may be produced, and sentic cycle therapy*, in *Emotion and psychopathology*. Plenum Press, 107–162.

Index

About the Author

Judith Pinkerton is a motivational speaker and facilitator of state board accredited music therapy workshops. Nurses, social workers, marriage and family therapists, alcohol and drug abuse counselors, and psychologists have attended her continuing education programs. Judith is in private practice as a music therapist. She also is a classically trained violinist whose performances over three decades have included classical, pop, jazz, and original therapeutic music. In 1990, she established The Center for Creative Therapeutic Arts, a nonprofit research and education center for the creative arts therapies.